CAPTAIN JOHN SMITH

WILLIAM PENN

JOEL CHANDLER HARRIS

SIR WALTER RALEIGH

GREAT EPOCHS IN AMERICAN HISTORY

DESCRIBED BY FAMOUS WRITERS

FROM COLUMBUS TO ROOSEVELT

Edited, with Introductions and Explanatory Notes

By FRANCIS W. HALSEY

Associate Editor of "The World's Famous Orations"; Associate Editor of "The Best of the World's Classics"; author of "The Old New York Frontier," etc.

PATRONS' EDITION. IN TEN VOLUMES
ILLUSTRATED

Vol. II

THE PLANTING OF THE FIRST COLONIES: 1562—1733

FUNK & WAGNALLS COMPANY

NEW YORK AND LONDON

INTRODUCTION

(The Planting of the First Colonies)

After the discoverers and explorers of the sixteenth century came (chiefly in the seventeenth) the founders of settlements that grew into States—French Huguenots in Florida and Carolina; Spaniards in St. Augustine; English Protestants in Virginia and Massachusetts; Dutch and English in New York; Swedes in New Jersey and Delaware; Catholic English in Maryland; Quaker English and Germans in Pennsylvania; Germans and Scotch-Irish in Carolina; French Catholics in Louisiana; Oglethorpe's debtors in Georgia.

To some of these came disastrous failures—to the Huguenots and Spaniards in Florida, to the English in Roanoke, Cuttyhunk and Kennebec. Others who survived had stern and precarious first years—the English in Jamestown and Plymouth, the Dutch in New York, the French in New Orleans. Chief among leaders stand John Smith, Bradford, Penn, Bienville and Oglethorpe, and chief among settlements, Jamestown, Plymouth, New York, Massachusetts Bay, Wilmington, Philadelphia, New Orleans and Savannah. The several movements, in their failures as in their successes, were distributed over a century and three-quarters, but since the coming of Columbus a much longer period had elapsed. From the discovery to the arrival of Oglethorpe lie 240 years, or a hundred years more than the period that separates our day from the years when America gained her independence from England.

Each center of settlement had been inspired by an impulse separate from that of others. Alike as some of them were, in having as a moving cause a desire to escape from persecution, religious or political, or otherwise to better conditions, they were divided by years, if not by generations, in time; the settlers came from lands isolated and remote from one another; they were different as to race, form of government, and religious and political ideals, and, once communities had been founded, each expanded on lines of its own and knew little of its neighbors.

The Spaniards who founded St. Augustine continued long to live there, but of social and political growth in Spanish Florida there was none. Spain, in those eventful European years, was fully absorbed elsewhere in Continental wars which taxed all her strength, especially that furious war, waged for forty years against Holland, and from which Spain retired ultimately in failure. In those years also was overthrown Philip's Armada, an event in which the scepter of maritime-empire passed from Spain to England.

Of the French settlements the chief was New Orleans, French from the beginning, and so to remain in racial preponderance, religious beliefs, and political ideals, for a century and a half after Bienville founded it—so, in fact, it still remains in our day. But elsewhere the French gave to the United States no permanent settlements. Numbers of them came to Florida, only to perish by the sword; others in large numbers settled in South Carolina, only to become merged with other races, among whom the English, with their speech and their laws, became supreme.

On Manhattan Island and in the valleys of the Hudson and lower Mohawk settled the Dutch a few years after the English at Jamestown. They erected forts on Manhattan Island and at Albany, Hartford and near Philadelphia; they partitioned vast tracts of fertile lands among favorite patroons; they built up a successful trade in furs with the Indians—and sent the profits home. Real settlements they did not found—at least, not settlements that were infused with the spirit of local enterprise, or animated by vital ambitions looking to growth in population and industry. After forty years of prosperity in trade they had failed to become a settled and well-ordered colonial state, looking bravely forward to permanence, expansion and eventual statehood. The first free school in America is credited to their initiative, and they were tolerant of other religions than their own, but they planted no other seeds from which a great State could grow.

As Coligny before him had sought to plant in Florida a colony of French Huguenots, so Raleigh, who had served under that great captain in the religious wars of the Continent, sought to found in Virginia a Protestant state. Much private wealth and many of his best years were given by Raleigh to the furtherance of a noble ambition, but all to futile immediate results. Raleigh's work, however, like all good work nobly done, was not lost. Out of his failure at Roanoke came English successes in later years—John Smith at Jamestown, the Pilgrims at Plymouth.

INTRODUCTION

Oldest of permanent English settlements in America is Jamestown, but the English failures at Cuttyhunk and Kennebec antedate it by a few years, and the failure at Roanoke by a quarter of a century. At Jamestown, ten years after the arrival of the first settlers, a legislative assembly was organized—a miniature parliament, modeled after the English House of Commons, and the first legislative body the new world ever knew. Here, too, in Jamestown began negro slavery in the United States, and in the same, or the next, year. Thus legislative freedom and human slavery had their beginning in America at the same time and in the same place.

Plymouth and Massachusetts Bay, next among the English settlements, followed in due time the failure of Gosnold at Cuttyhunk and the description of New England John Smith wrote and printed in 1614 after a voyage of exploration along her coast. After several years Plymouth contained only about 300 souls, but the Bay colony, founded ten years later, increased rapidly. By 1634 nearly 4,000 of Winthrop's followers had arrived, many of them college graduates. From this great parent colony went forth Roger Williams to Rhode Island, Hooker to Hartford, Davenport to New Haven, so that by the middle of the seventeenth century five English colonies had been planted within the borders of New England.

Long after all these came the Maryland and Pennsylvania settlements, founded by Lord Baltimore and William Penn as lords proprietor, owners of vast tracts of land and possessing privileges more extensive than ever before were bestowed on British subjects. In the new century arrived Oglethorpe, with his insolvent debtors, soon to find Spaniards from St. Augustine hostile to his enterprise. But Oglethorpe was a soldier as well as a colonizer; he had served in Continental wars, and, after laying siege to St. Augustine further aggressions from that source ceased.

Thus at last, in the New World, the English race, their flag, their language and their laws, had displaced the Spaniards in that world-important contest for dominion and power, of which the second issue was soon to be fought out on many bloody fields with France.

F. W. H.

CONTENTS

CONTENTS

THE PLANTING OF THE FIRST COLONIES

COLONIES

1562—1733

THE FOUNDING OF ST. AUGUSTINE AND THE MASSACRE BY MENENDEZ

(1562—1565)

I.

THE ACCOUNT BY JOHN A. DOYLE[1]

In 1562 the French Huguenot party, headed by Coligny, made another attempt[2] to secure themselves a refuge in the New World. Two ships set sail under the command of Jean Ribault, a brave and experienced seaman, destined to play a memorable and tragic part in the history of America. Ribault does not seem to have set out with any definite scheme of colonization, but rather, like Amidas and Barlow, to have contented himself

---

[1] From Doyle's "English Colonies in America." By permission of the publishers, Henry Holt & Co.

[2] Coligny's first attempt was made in 1555, when two shiploads of Huguenot immigrants (290 persons), under Villegagnon, were sent to Brazil. This settlement was soon destroyed by the Portuguese.

Menendez's expedition of 1565 followed the earlier Spanish expeditions by Ponce de Leon, Narvaez and De Soto. It sailed from Cadiz and comprized eleven ships. Twenty-three other vessels followed, the entire company numbering 2,646 persons. The aim of Menendez was to begin a permanent settlement in Florida. On arrival he found a colony of

with preliminary exploration. In April he landed on the coast of Florida. . . .

After he had laid the foundations of a fort, called in honor of the king Charlefort, Ribault returned to France. He would seem to have been unfortunate in his choice alike of colonists and of a commander. The settlers lived on the charity of the Indians, sharing in their festivities, wandering from village to village and wholly doing away with any belief in their superior wisdom and power which might yet have possest their savage neighbors. . . .

France was torn asunder by civil war, and had no leisure to think of an insignificant settlement beyond the Atlantic. No supplies came to the settlers, and they could not live forever on the bounty of their savage neighbors. The settlers decided to return home. To do this it was needful to build a bark with their own hands from the scanty resources which the wilderness offered. Whatever might have been the failings of the settlers, they certainly showed no lack of energy or of skill in concerting means for their departure. They felled the trees to make planks, moss served for calking, and their shirts and

French Huguenots already in possession, having been there three years. A conflict was inevitable, and one which forms a most melancholy chapter in the early history of American colonization. Menendez hanged Huguenots, "not as Frenchmen, but as heretics," while Gourgues hanged Spaniards "not as Spaniards, but as traitors, robbers and murderers." After the conflicts closed the Spaniards maintained themselves in St. Augustine until 1586, when St. Augustine was completely destroyed by Sir Francis Drake. Two years later the Armada of Spain was overthrown in the English Channel, largely as the work of Drake.

bedding for sails, while their Indian friends supplied cordage. When their bark was finished they set sail. Unluckily in their impatience to be gone, they did not reckon what supplies they would need. The wind, at first favorable, soon turned against them, and famine stared them in the face. Driven to the last resort of starving seamen, they cast lots for a victim, and the lot, by a strange chance, fell upon the very man whose punishment had been a chief count against De Pierria. Life was supported by this hideous relief, till they came in sight of the French coast. Even then their troubles were not over. An English privateer bore down upon them and captured them. The miseries of the prisoners seem, in some measure, to have touched their enemies. A few of the weakest were landed on French soil. The rest ended their wanderings in an English prison.

The needs of the abandonment of the colony did not reach France till long after the event. Before its arrival a fleet was sent out to the relief of the colony. Three ships were dispatched, the largest of a hundred and twenty tons, the least of sixty tons, under the command of René Laudonnière, a young Poitevin of good birth. On their outward voyage they touched at Teneriffe and Dominica, and found ample evidence at each place of the terror which the Spaniards had inspired among the natives. In June the French reached the American shore south of Port Royal. As before, their reception by the Indians was friendly. Some further exploration failed to discover a more suitable site than that which had first presented itself, and accordingly a wooden fort was soon built with a timber palisade and bastions of earthen work. Before long the newcomers found that their intercourse with the Indians was attended with unlooked-for difficulties. There were three tribes of importance, each under the command of a single chief, and all more or less hostile to the other. In the South the power of the chiefs seems to have been far more dreaded, and their influence over the national policy more authoritative than among the tribes of New England and Canada. Laudonnière, with questionable judgment, entangled himself in these Indian feuds, and entered into an offensive alliance with the first of these chiefs whom he encountered, Satouriona. . . .

A new source of trouble, however, soon beset the unhappy colonists. Their quarrels had left them no time for tilling the soil, and they were wholly dependent on the Indians for food. The friendship of the savages soon proved but a precarious means of support. The dissensions in the French camp must have lowered the new-comers in the eyes of their savage neighbors. They would only part with their supplies on exorbitant terms. Laudonnière himself throughout would have adopted moderate and conciliatory measures, but his men at length became impatient and seized one of the principal Indian chiefs as a hostage for the good behavior of his countrymen. A skirmish ensued, in which the French were victorious. It was clear, however, that the settlement could not continue to depend on supplies extorted from the Indians at the point of the sword. The settlers felt that they were wholly forgotten by their friends in France, and they

6

decided, tho with heavy hearts, to forsake the country which they had suffered so much to win. . . .

Just, however, as all the preparations for departure were made, the long-expected help came. Ribault arrived from France with a fleet of seven vessels containing three hundred settlers and ample supplies. This arrival was not a source of unmixed joy to Laudonnière. His factious followers had sent home calumnious reports about him, and Ribault brought out orders to send him home to stand his trial. Ribault himself seems to have been easily persuaded of the falsity of the charges, and prest Laudonnière to keep his command; but he, broken in spirit and sick in body, declined to resume office.

All disputes soon disappeared in the face of a vast common misfortune. Whatever internal symptoms of weakness might already display themselves in the vast fabric of the Spanish empire, its rulers showed as yet no lack of jealous watchfulness against any attempts to rival her successes in America. The attempts of Cartier and Roberval[3] had been watched, and the Spanish ambassador at Lisbon had proposed to the King of Portugal to send out a joint armament to dispossess the intruders. The king deemed the danger too remote to be worth an expedition, and the Spaniards unwillingly acquiesced. An outpost of fur traders in the ice-bound wilderness of Canada might seem to bring little danger with it. But a settlement on the coast of Florida, within some eight days' sail of Havana, with a har-

[3] In the valley of the St. Lawrence as described in Volume I.

bor whence privateers might waylay Spanish ships and even attack Spanish colonies, was a rival not to be endured. Moreover, the colonists were not only foreigners but Huguenots, and their heresy served at once as a pretext and stimulus to Spanish zeal.

The man to whose lot it fell to support the monopoly of Spain against French aggression was one who, if we may judge by his American career, needed only a wider field to rival the genius and the atrocities of Alva. Pedro de Menendez, when he had scarcely passed from boyhood, had fought both against the French and the Turks, and had visited America and returned laden with wealth. He then did good service in command of the Spanish fleet in the French war, and his prompt co-operation with the land force gave him a share in the glories of St. Quentin.[4] A second voyage to America was even more profitable than the first, but his misconduct there brought him into conflict with the Council of the Indies, by whom he was imprisoned, and heavily fined. His previous services, however, had gained him the favor of the court. Part of his fine was remitted, and he was emboldened to ask not merely for pardon, but for promotion. He proposed to revive the attempt of De Soto and to extend the Spanish power over Florida. The expedition was to be at Menendez's own cost; he was to take out five hundred colonists, and in return to be made Governor of Florida for life and to enjoy certain

[4] St. Quentin is a town in northeastern France, near which on August 10, 1557, the army of Philip II, Spain, won a great victory over the combined armies of France and England.

rights for free trade with the West Indies and with the mother country. . . .

The military genius of Menendez rose to the new demands made upon it. He at once decided on a bold and comprehensive scheme which would secure the whole coast from Port Royal to Chesapeake Bay, and would ultimately give Spain exclusive possession of the South Seas and the Newfoundland fisheries. The Spanish captain had a mind which could at once conceive a wide scheme and labor at the execution of details. So resolutely were operations carried on that by June, 1565, Menendez sailed from Cadiz with thirty-four vessels and four thousand six hundred men. After a stormy voyage he reached the mouth of the St. John's river. Ribault's party was about to land, and some of the smaller vessels had crossed the harbor, while others yet stood out to sea. Menendez hailed the latter, and after some parley told them that he had come there with orders from the king of Spain to kill all intruders that might be found on the coast. The French being too few to fight, fled. Menendez did not for the present attack the settlement, but sailed southward till he reached a harbor which he named St. Augustine. There the Spaniards disembarked and threw up a fortification destined to grow into the town of St. Augustine, the first permanent Spanish settlement north of the Gulf of Mexico. Various attempts had been made, and with various motives. The slave-hunter, the gold-seeker, the explorer had each tried his fortunes in Florida, and each failed. The difficulties which had baffled them all were at length overcome by the spirit of religious hatred.

Meanwhile a council of war was sitting at the French settlement, Charlefort. Ribault, contrary to the wishes of Laudonnière and the rest, decided to anticipate the Spaniards by an attack from the sea. A few sick men were left with Laudonnière to garrison the fort; all the rest went on board. Just as everything was ready for the attack, a gale sprang up, and the fleet of Ribault, instead of bearing down on St. Augustine, was straggling in confusion off an unknown and perilous coast. Menendez, relieved from immediate fear for his own settlement, determined on a bold stroke. Like Ribault, he bore down the opposition of a cautious majority, and with five hundred picked men marched overland through thirty miles of swamp and jungle against the French fort. Thus each commander was exposing his own settlement in order to menace his enemies.

In judging, however, of the relative prudence of the two plans, it must be remembered that an attack by land is far more under control, and far less liable to be disarranged by unforeseen chances than one by sea. At first it seemed as if each expedition was destined to the same fate. The weather was as unfavorable to the Spanish by land as to the French by sea. At one time a mutiny was threatened, but Menendez succeeded in inspiring his men with something of his own enthusiasm, and they persevered. Led by a French deserter, they approached the unprotected settlement. So stormy was the night that the sentinels had left the walls. The fort was stormed; Laudonnière and a few others escaped to the shore and were picked up by one of Ribault's vessels returning from its unsuccessful expedition. The rest, to the number of one hundred and forty, were slain in the attack or taken prisoners. The women and children were spared, the men were hung on trees with an inscription pinned to their breasts: "Not as to Frenchmen. but as to Lutherans."

The fate of Ribault's party was equally wretched. All were shipwrecked, but most apparently succeeded in landing alive. Then began a scene of deliberate butchery, aggravated, if the French accounts may be believed, by the most shameless treachery. As the scattered bands of shipwrecked men wandered through the forest, seeking to return to Fort Caroline, they were mercilessly entrapped by friendly words, if not by explicit promises of safety. Some escaped to the Indians, a few were at last spared by the contemptuous mercy of the foes. Those of the survivors who profest themselves converts were pardoned, the rest were sent to the galleys. Ribault himself was among the murdered. If we may believe the story current in France, his head, sawn in four parts, was set up over the corners of the fort of St. Augustine, while a piece of his beard was sent as a trophy to the king of Spain. . . .

Dominic de Gourgues had already known as a prisoner of war the horrors of the Spanish galleys. Whether he was a Huguenot is uncertain. Happily in France, as the history of that and all later ages proved, the religion of the Catholic did not necessarily deaden the feelings of the patriot. Seldom has there been a deed of more reckless daring than that which Dominic de Gourgues now undertook. With the proceeds of his patrimony he bought three small ships, manned by eighty sailors and a hundred men-at-arms. He then obtained a commission as a slaver on the coast of Guinea, and in the summer of 1567 set sail. With these paltry resources he aimed at overthrowing a settlement which had already destroyed a force of twenty times his number, and which might have been strengthened in the interval. . . .

Three days were spent in making ready, and then De Gourgues, with a hundred and sixty of his own men and his Indian allies, marched against the enemy. In spite of the hostility of the Indians the Spaniards seem to have taken no precaution against a sudden attack. Menendez himself had left the colony. The Spanish force was divided between three forts, and no proper precautions were taken for keeping up the communications between them. Each was successively seized, the garrison slain or made prisoners, and as each fort fell those in the next could only make vague guesses as to the extent of the danger. Even when divided into three the Spanish force outnumbered that of De Gourgues, and savages with bows and arrows would have counted for little against men with firearms and behind walls. But after the downfall of the first fort a panic seemed to seize the Spaniards, and the French achieved an almost bloodless victory. After the death of Ribault and his followers nothing could be looked for but merciless retaliation, and De Gourgues copied the severity, though not the perfidy, of his enemies. The very details of Menendez's act were imitated, and the trees on which the prisoners were hung bore the inscription: "Not as Spaniards, but as traitors, robbers, and mur-

derers." Five weeks later De Gourgues anchored
under the walls of Rochelle, and that noble city,
where civil and religious freedom found a home
in their darkest hour, received him with the
honor he deserved.

II

MENDOZA'S ACCOUNT OF THE MASSACRE[1]

We saw two islands, called the Bahama Islands.
The shoals which lie between them are so extensive that the billows are felt far out at sea.
The general gave orders to take soundings. The
ship purchased at Porto Rico got aground that
day in two and a half fathoms of water. At first
we feared she might stay there; but she soon got
off and came to us. Our galley, one of the best
ships afloat, found herself all day in the same
position, when suddenly her keel struck three
times violently against the bottom. The sailors
gave themselves up for lost, and the water com-
menced to pour into her hold. But, as we had
a mission to fulfil for Jesus Christ and His blessed
mother, two heavy waves, which struck her abaft,
set her afloat again, and soon after we found her
in deep water, and at midnight we entered the
Bahama Channel.

On Saturday, the 25th, the captain-general
(Menendez) came to visit our vessel and get the

[1] Francisco Lopez de Mendoza was the chaplain of the expedition. His account is printed in "Old South Leaflets."

ordnance for disembarkment at Florida. This ordnance consisted of two rampart pieces, of two sorts of culverins, of very small caliber, powder and balls; and he also took two soldiers to take care of the pieces. Having armed his vessel, he stopt and made us an address, in which he instructed us what we had to do on arrival at the place where the French were anchored. I will not dwell on this subject, on which there was a good deal said for and against, although the opinion of the general finally prevailed. There were two thousand (hundred) Frenchmen in the seaport into which we were to force an entrance. I made some opposition to the plans, and begged the general to consider that he had the care of a thousand souls, for which he must give a good account. . . .

On Tuesday, the 4th, we took a northerly course, keeping all the time close to the coast. On Wednesday, the 5th, two hours before sunset, we saw four French ships at the mouth of a river.[2] When we were two leagues from them the first galley joined the rest of the fleet, which was composed of four other vessels. The general concerted a plan with the captains and pilots, and ordered the flag-ship, the *San Pelayo,* and a *chaloupe* to attack the French flag-ship, the *Trinity,* while the first galley and another *chaloupe* would attack the French galley, both of which vessels were very large and powerful. All the ships of our fleet put

---

[2] These ships, commanded by Ribault,—seven in number, with 500 men besides families of artizans on board,—had arrived at the mouth of the St. John's River on August 29, 1565. The four left outside, as seen by Menendez, were at the time disembarking their passengers.

themselves in good position; the troops were in the best of spirits, and full of confidence in the great talents of the captain-general. They followed the galley; but, as our general is a very clever and artful officer, he did not fire, nor seek to make any attack on the enemy. He went straight to the French galley, and cast anchor about eight paces from her. The other vessels went to the windward, and very near the enemy. During the maneuvers, which lasted until about two hours after sunset, not a word was said on either side. Never in my life have I known such stillness. Our general inquired of the French galley, which was the vessel nearest his, "Whence does this fleet come?" They answered, "From France." "What are you doing here?" said the Adelantado. "This is the territory of King Philip II. I order you to leave directly; for I neither know who you are nor what you want here."

The French commander then replied, "I am bringing soldiers and supplies to the fort of the King of France." He then asked the name of the general of our fleet, and was told, "Pedro Menendez de Aviles, Captain-general of the King of Spain, who have come to hang all Lutherans I find here." Our general then asked him the name of his commander, and he replied, "Lord Gasto." While this parleying was going on, a long-boat was sent from the galley to the flag-ship. The person charged with this errand managed to do it so secretly that we could not hear what was said; but we understood the reply of the French to be, "I am the admiral," which made us think he wished to surrender, as they were in so small a force. Scarcely had the French made this reply, when they slipped their cables, spread their sails, and passed through our midst. Our admiral, seeing this, followed the French commander, and called upon him to lower his sails, in the name of King Philip, to which he received an impertinent answer. Immediately our admiral gave an order to discharge a small culverin, the ball from which struck the vessel amidship, and I thought she was going to founder. We gave chase, and some time after he again called on them to lower their sails. "I would sooner die first than surrender!" replied the French commander. The order was given to fire a second shot, which carried off five or six men; but, as these miserable devils are very good sailors, they maneuvered so well that we could not take one of them; and, notwithstanding all the guns we fired at them, we did not sink one of their ships. We only got possession of one of their large boats, which was of great service to us afterward. During the whole night our flag-ship (the *San Pelayo*) and the galley chased the French flag-ship (*Trinity*) and galley. . . .

The next morning, being fully persuaded that the storm had made a wreck of our galley, or that, at least, she had been driven a hundred leagues out to sea, we decided that so soon as daylight came we would weigh anchor, and withdraw in good order, to a river (Seloy) which was below the French colony, and there disembark, and construct a fort, which we would defend until assistance came to us.

On Thursday, just as day appeared, we sailed toward the vessel at anchor, passed very close to her, and would certainly have captured her, when

we saw another vessel appear on the open sea,
which we thought was one of ours. At the same
moment, however, we thought we recognized the
French admiral's ship. We perceived the ship
on the open sea: it was the French galley of which
we had been in pursuit. Finding ourselves between these two vessels, we decided to direct our
course toward the galley, for the sake of deceiv-
ing them and preventing them from attacking us,
so as not to give them any time to wait. This bold
maneuver having succeeded, we sought the river
Seloy and port, of which I have spoken, where
we had the good fortune to find our galley, and
another vessel which had planned the same thing
we had. Two companies of infantry now disembarked: that of Captain Andres Soyez Patino,
and that of Captain Juan de San Vincente, who
is a very distinguished gentleman. They were well
received by the Indians, who gave them a large
house belonging to a chief, and situated near the
shore of a river. Immediately Captain Patino
and Captain San Vincente, both men of talent
and energy, ordered an intrenchment to be built
around this house, with a slope of earth and fas-
cines, these being the only means of defense possible in that country, where stones are nowhere
to be found. Up to to-day we have disembarked
twenty-four pieces of bronze guns of different cali-
bers, of which the least weighed fifteen hundred
weight. Our fort is at a distance of about fifteen leagues from that of the enemy (Fort Carolin). The energy and talents of those two brave
captains, joined to the efforts of their brave soldiers, who had no tools with which to work the
earth, accomplished the construction of this fort-

ress of defence; and, when the general disembarked he was quite surprized with what had been done.

On Saturday, the 8th, the general landed with many banners spread, to the sound of trumpets and salutes of artillery. As I had gone ashore the evening before, I took a cross and went to meet him, singing the hymn *Te Deum laudamus.* The general marched up to the cross, followed by all who accompanied him, and there they all kneeled and embraced the cross. A large number of Indians watched these proceedings and imitated all they saw done. The same day the general took formal possession of the country in the name of his Majesty, and all the captains took the oath of allegiance to him, as their general and governor of the country. . . .

Our general was very bold in all military matters, and a great enemy of the French. He immediately assembled his captains and planned an expedition to attack the French settlement and fort on the river with five hundred men; and, in spite of the opinion of a majority of them, and of my judgment and of another priest, he ordered his plan to be carried out. Accordingly, on Monday, September 17, he set out with five hundred men, well provided with fire-arms and pikes, each soldier carrying with him a sack of bread and supply of wine for the journey. They also took with them two Indian chiefs, who were the implacable enemies of the French, to serve as guides. . . .

I have previously stated that our brave captain-general set out on the 17th of September with five hundred arquebusiers and pikemen, under the guidance of two Indian chiefs, who showed them the route to the enemy's fort. They marched the whole distance until Tuesday evening, the 18th of September, 1565, when they arrived within a quarter of a league of the enemy's fort (Carolin), where they remained all night up to their waists in water. When daylight came, Captains Lopez, Patino, and Martin Ochoa had already been to examine the fort, but, when they went to attack the fort, a greater part of the soldiers were so confused they scarcely knew what they were about.

On Thursday morning our good captain-general, accompanied by his son-in-law, Don Pedro de Valdes, and Captain Patino, went to inspect the fort. He showed so much vivacity that he did not seem to have suffered by any of the hardships to which he had been exposed, and, seeing him march off so brisk, the others took courage, and without exception followed his example. It appears the enemy did not perceive their approach until the very moment of the attack, as it was very early in the morning and had rained in torrents. The greater part of the soldiers of the fort were still in bed. Some arose in their shirts, and others, quite naked, begged for quarter; but, in spite of that, more than one hundred and forty were killed. A great Lutheran cosmographer and magician was found among the dead. The rest, numbering about three hundred, scaled the walls, and either took refuge in the forest or on their ships floating in the river, laden with treasures, so that in an hour's time the fort was in our possession, without our having lost a single man, or even had one wounded. There were six vessels on the river at the time. They took one brig, and an unfinished galley and another vessel, which had been just discharged of a load of rich merchandise, and sunk. These vessels were placed at the entrance to the bar to blockade the harbor, as they expected we would come by sea. Another, laden with wine and merchandise, was near the port. She refused to surrender, and spread her sails, when they fired on her from the fort, and sunk her in a spot where neither the vessel nor cargo will be lost.

The taking of this fort gained us many valuable objects, namely, two hundred pikes, a hundred and twenty helmets, a quantity of arquebuses and shields, a quantity of clothing, linen, fine cloths, two hundred tons of flour, a good many barrels of biscuit, two hundred bushels of wheat, three horses, four asses, and two she-asses, hogs, tallow, books, furnace, flour-mill, and many other things of little value. But the greatest advantage of this victory is certainly the triumph which our Lord has granted us, and which will be the means of the holy Gospel being introduced into this country, a thing necessary to prevent the loss of many souls. . . .

When we had reached the sea, we went about three leagues along the coast in search of our comrades. It was about ten o'clock at night when we met them, and there was a mutual rejoicing at having found each other. Not far off we saw the camp fires of our enemies, and our general ordered two of our soldiers to go and reconnoiter them, concealing themselves in the bushes, and to observe well the ground where they were encamped, so as to know what could be done. About two o'clock the men returned, saying that the enemy was on the other side of the river, and that we could not get at them. Immediately the general

ordered two soldiers and four sailors to return to
where we had left the boats, and bring them down
the river, so that we might pass over to where the
enemy was. Then he marched his troops forward
to the river, and we arrived before daylight. We
concealed ourselves in a hollow between the sand-
hills, with the Indians who were with us; and,
when it became light, we saw a great many of the
enemy go down to the river to get shell-fish for
food. Soon after we saw a flag hoisted, as a war-
signal.

Our general, who was observing all that, en-
lightened by the Holy Spirit, said to us, "I intend to change these clothes for those of a sailor,
and take a Frenchman with me (one of those
whom we had brought with us from Spain), and
we will go and talk with these Frenchmen. Perhaps they are without supplies, and would be glad
to surrender without fighting." He had scarcely
finished speaking before he put his plan into execution. As soon as he had called to them, one
of them swam toward and spoke to him; told
him of their having been shipwrecked, and the distress they were in; that they had not eaten bread
for eight or ten days; and, what is more, stated
that all, or at least the greater part of them, were
Lutherans. Immediately the general sent him
back to his countrymen, to say they must surrender, and give up their arms, or he would put
them all to death. A French gentleman, who was
a sergeant, brought back the reply that they would
surrender on condition their lives should be spared.
After having parleyed a long time, our brave captain-general answered "that he would make no
promises, that they must surrender uncondition-

21

ally, and lay down their arms, because, if he spared their lives, he wanted them to be grateful for it, and, if they were put to death, that there should be no cause for complaint." Seeing that there was nothing else left for them to do, the sergeant returned to the camp; and soon after he brought all their arms and flags, and gave them up to the general, and surrendered unconditionally. Finding they were all Lutherans, the captain-general ordered them all to be put to death; but, as I was a priest, and had bowels of mercy, I begged him to grant me the favor of sparing those whom we might find to be Christians. He granted it; and I made investigations, and found ten or twelve of the men Roman Catholics, whom we brought back. All the others were executed, because they were Lutherans and enemies of our Holy Catholic faith. All this took place on Saturday (St. Michael's Day), September 29, 1565.[3]

[3] When the French Government learned of this massacre, the event did not arouse any particular interest. Indeed, the colony seems not to have had any special protection from the home authorities. Had the contrary been the case, it would have been easily possible for the French to have built up a flourishing colony in America nearly half a century before the English were ever established in the new world.

SIR WALTER RALEIGH'S VIRGINIA COLONIES

(1584—1587)

I

THE ACCOUNT BY JOHN A. DOYLE[1]

The task in which Gilbert[2] had failed was to be undertaken by one better qualified to carry it out. If any Englishman in that age seemed to be marked out as the founder of a colonial empire, it was Raleigh. Like Gilbert, he had studied books; like Drake, he could rule men. The pupil of Coligny, the friend of Spenser, traveler-soldier, scholar, courtier, statesman, Raleigh with all his varied graces and powers rises before us, the type and personification of the age in which he lived. The associations of his youth, and the training of his early manhood, fitted him to sympathize with the aims of his half-brother Gilbert, and there is little reason to doubt that Raleigh had a share in his undertaking and his failure.

[1] From Doyle's "English Colonies in America." By permission of the publishers, Henry Holt & Co.

[2] Sir Humphrey Gilbert, a half-brother of Raleigh, is here referred to. In 1578 he had obtained royal permission to found a colony in America, but his expedition, after starting, turned back, a failure. In 1583 he again set out, landing at St. John's, Newfoundland, where he established the first English colony in North America. On returning home his ship was lost in a storm off the Azores.

In 1584 he obtained a patent precisely similar to Gilbert's. His first step showed the thoughtful and well-planned system on which he began his task. Two ships were sent out, not with any idea of settlement, but to examine and report upon the country. Their commanders were Arthur Barlow and Philip Amidas. To the former we owe the extant record of the voyage: the name of the latter would suggest that he was a foreigner. Whether by chance or design, they took a more southerly course than any of their predecessors. . . .

Coasting along for about a hundred and twenty miles the voyagers reached an inlet and with some difficulty entered. They solemnly took possession of the land in the Queen's name, and then delivered it over to Raleigh according to his patent. They soon discovered that the land upon which they had touched was an island about twenty miles long and not above six broad, named, as they afterward learned, Roanoke. Beyond, separating them from the mainland, lay an enclosed sea, studded with more than a hundred fertile and well-wooded islets. . . .

Barlow and Amidas returned to England in the middle of September. With them they brought two of the savages, named Wanchese and Manteo. A probable tradition tells us that the Queen herself named the country Virginia, and that Raleigh's knighthood was the reward and acknowledgement of his success. On the strength of this report Raleigh at once made preparations for a settlement. A fleet of seven ships was provided for the conveyance of a hundred and eight settlers. The fleet was under the command of Sir Richard Grenville, who was to establish the settlement and leave it under the charge of Ralph Lane. . . .

On the 20th of June the fleet reached the coast of Florida, and three days later narrowly escaped being cast away off Cape Fear. In a few days more they anchored at Wococon, an island near Roanoke. In entering the harbor the largest ship, the *Tiger*, struck a sand-bar, and was nearly lost, either through the clumsiness or treachery of the pilot, Simon Fernando, a Portuguese. On the 11th of July Grenville, with forty others, including Lane, Amidas, and the chief men of the expedition, crossed over to the mainland. Taking a northerly direction, they explored the coast as far as Secotan, an Indian town some sixty miles south of Roanoke, where they were hospitably received by the savages. It is melancholy, after the bright picture of the intercourse between the natives and the English drawn by Barlow, to have to record hostilities, in which by far the greater share of blame lay with our countrymen. On the voyage back to Roanoke a silver cup was stolen from the English at one of the Indian villages. In revenge the English put the inhabitants to flight, burnt the village and destroyed the crops. On the 3d of August one ship sailed home, and on the 25th Grenville left the colony, followed, as it would seem, during the course of the next month by the rest of the fleet.[3] . . .

The site of the settlement was at the northeast corner of the island of Roanoke, whence the settlers could command the strait. There, even now, choked by vines and underwood, and here and

[3] See in the next chapter an account of Lane's return with Drake.

there broken by the crumbling remains of an earthen bastion, may be traced the outlines of the ditch which enclosed the camp, some forty yards square, the home of the first English settlers in the New World. . . .

If the failure of his colony was likely to deter Raleigh from further efforts, this was more than outweighed by the good report of the country given both by Lane and Heriot. Accordingly, in the very next year, Raleigh put out another and a larger expedition under the leadership of John White. The constitution of White's expedition would seem to show that it was designed to be more a colony, properly speaking, than Lane's settlement at Roanoke. A government was formed by Raleigh, consisting of White and twelve others, incorporated as the governor and assistants of the city of Raleigh. Of the hundred and fifty settlers seventeen were women, of whom seven seem to have been unmarried. The emigrants evidently did not go as mere explorers or adventurers; they were to be the seed of a commonwealth. . . .

On the 2d of July the fleet reached Haterask, the port at which Grenville had landed on his last voyage. There White took fifty men ashore to search for the fifteen whom Grenville had left there. They found nothing but the bones of one man, slain, as they afterward learned, by the Indians. The rest had disappeared, and it was not till some time afterward that their countrymen learned any tidings of their fate. Ignorant, no doubt, of the altered feelings of the natives, Grenville's men had lived carelessly, and kept no watch. Pemissapan's warriors had seized the opportunity to revenge the death of their chief, and had sent a party of thirty men against the English settlement. Two of the chief men were sent forward to demand a parley with two of the English. The latter fell into the trap, and sent out two of their number. One of these was instantly seized and killed, whereupon the other fled. The thirty Indians then rushed out and fired the house, in which the English settlers took refuge. The English, thus dislodged, forced their way out, losing one man in the skirmish, and at last, after being sorely prest by the arrows of their enemies, and by their skill in fighting behind covert, they reached the boat and escaped to Haterask. After this neither Indians nor English ever heard of them again. . . .

A more hopeful omen might be drawn from the birth of a child five days later, the first born to English parents in the New World. Her father, Ananias Dare, was one of the twelve assistants, and her mother, Eleanor, was the daughter of John White. Each event, the birth of Virginia Dare, the baptism and ennobling of Manteo, was trivial in itself, yet when brought together, the contrast gives a solemn meaning. It seemed as if within five days the settlement of Roanoke had seen an old world pass away, a new world born.

In August White wished to send home two of the assistants to represent the state of the colony, but, for some reason, none of them were willing to go. The wish of the colony generally seemed to be that White himself should undertake the mission. After some demur, chiefly on the ground that his own private interests required his presence in the settlement, White assented, and on the 27th of August he sailed. . . .

Soon after White's return Raleigh fitted out a fleet under the command of Grenville. Before that fleet could sail Raleigh and Grenville were called off to a task even more pressing than the relief of the Virginia plantation. Yet, notwithstanding the prospect of a Spanish invasion, White persuaded Raleigh to send out two small vessels, with which White himself sailed from Bideford on the 25th of April, 1588. The sailors, however, fell into the snare so often fatal to the explorers of that age. In the words of a later writer, whose vigorous language seemed to have been borrowed from some contemporary chronicler, the captains, "being more intent on a gainful voyage than the relief of the colony, ran in chase of prizes; till at last one of them, meeting two ships of war, was, after a bloody fight, overcome, boarded and rifled. In this maimed, ransacked, and ragged condition she returned to England in a month's time; and in about three weeks after the other also returned, having perhaps tasted of the same fare, at least without performing her intended voyage, to the distress, and, as it proved, the utter destruction of the colony of Virginia, and to the great displeasure of their patron at home."

Raleigh had now spent forty thousand pounds on the colonization of Virginia, with absolutely no return. In March, 1589, he made an assignment, granting to Sir Thomas Smith, White and others the privilege of trading in Virginia, while he proved at the same time that he had not lost his interest in the undertaking by a gift of a hundred pounds for the conversion of the natives. The unhappy colonists gained nothing by the change. For a whole year no relief was sent. When, at

length, White sailed with three ships, he or his
followers imitated the folly of their predecessors,
and preferred buccaneering among the Spaniards
in the West Indies to conveying immediate relief
to the colonists. On their arrival nothing was to
be seen of the settlers. After some search the
name Croaton was seen carved on a post, according to an arrangement made with White before
his departure, by which the settlers were thus to
indicate the course they had taken. Remnants of
their goods were found, but no trace of the settlers themselves. Years afterward, when Virginia had been at length settled by Englishmen,
a faint tradition found its way among them of a
band of white captives, who, after being for years
kept by the Indians in laborious slavery, were at
length massacred. Such were the only tidings of
Raleigh's colonists that ever reached the ears of
their countrymen. White, with his three ships, returned, and the colonization of Virginia was for
a time at an end. Even Raleigh's indomitable
spirit gave way, and he seems henceforth to have
abandoned all hope of a plantation. Yet he did
not, till after fifteen years of disappointment and
failure, give up the search for his lost settlers.
Before he died the great work of his life had been
accomplished, but by other hands. In spite of the
intrigues of the Spanish court and the scoffs of
playwrights, Virginia had been settled and had
become a flourishing colony. A ship had sailed
into London laden with Virginia goods, and an
Indian princess,[4] the wife of an Englishman, had

---

[4] Pocahontas, married to John Rolfe, went to England with
Rolfe and there died about a year later. She left a son
who returned to Virginia, where he left descendants, among

been received at court, and had for a season furnished wonder and amusement to the fashionable world.

II

THE RETURN OF THE COLONISTS WITH SIR FRANCIS DRAKE

(1586)

BY RALPH LANE[1]

This fell out the first of June, 1586, and the eight of the same came advertisement to me from captaine Stafford, lying at my lord Admirals Island, that he had discovered a great fleet of three and twentie sailes: but whether they were friends or foes, he could not yet discerne. He advised me to stand upon as good guard as I could.

The ninth of the sayd moneth he himselfe came unto me, having that night before, and that same day travelled by land twenty miles: and I must truely report of him from the first to the last; hee

whom was the famous John Randolph of Roanoke. John Smith's account of the saving of his life by Pocahontas is printed in Volume I of "The Best of the World's Classics."

[1] Ralph Lane went out to Virginia in 1585 with the ships dispatched in that year by Raleigh and commanded by Sir Richard Grenville, the company numbering one hundred householders. After landing at Roanoke, Grenville returned to England for supplies, leaving the colony in charge of Lane. Lane has left an important account of the experiences and sufferings of the colonists during the absence of

was the gentleman that never spared labour or perill either by land or water, faire weather or foule, to performe any service committed unto him.

He brought me a letter from the Generall Sir Francis Drake, with a most bountifull and honourable offer for the supply of our necessities to the performance of the action wee were entred into; and that not only of victuals, munition, and clothing, but also of barks, pinnesses, and boats; they also by him to be victualled, manned and furnished to my contentation.

The tenth day he arrived in the road of our bad harborow: and comming there to an anker, the eleventh day I came to him, whom I found in deeds most honourably to performe that which in writing and message he had most curteously offered, he having aforehand propounded the matter of all the captaines of his fleet, and got their liking and consent thereto.

With such thanks unto him and his captaines for his care both of us and of our action, not as the matter deserved, but as I could both for my company and myselfe, I (being aforehand prepared what I would desire) craved at his hands that it would please him to take with him into

Grenville, whose return was delayed. Drake, meanwhile coming up from St. Augustine, which he had just destroyed, put in at Roanoke in 1586, and the whole company returned to England with him. Grenville afterward arrived in Roanoke, finding no one there. He then returned to England, leaving on the island fifteen men. In the following year Raleigh sent out to Roanoke John White. When White arrived he found that these men had all been massacred by the Indians. Other expeditions were sent out later, but none was able to establish any colony at Roanoke. Lane's account is printed in "Old South Leaflets."

England a number of weake and unfit men for any good action, which I would deliver to him; and in place of them to supply me of his company with oare-men, artificers, and others.

That he would leave us so much shipping and victuall, as about August then next following would cary me and all my company into England, when we had discovered somewhat, that for lacke of needfull provision in time left with us as yet remained undone.

That it woulde please him withall to leave some sufficient Masters not onely to cary us into England, when time should be, but also to search the coast for some better harborow, if there were any, and especially to helpe us to some small boats and oare-men. Also for a supply of calievers, hand weapons, match and lead, tooles, apparell, and such like.

He having received these my requests, according to his usuall commendable maner of government (as it was told me) calling his captains to counsell; the resolution was that I should send such of my officers of my company as I used in such matters, with their notes, to goe aboord with him; which were the Master of the victuals, the Keeper of the store, and the Vicetreasurer: to whom he appointed forthwith for me *The Francis*, being a very proper barke of 70 tun, and tooke present order for bringing of victual aboord her for 100 men for foure moneths, with all my other demands whatsoever, to the uttermost.

And further, he appointed for me two pinnesses, and foure small boats: and that which was to performe all his former liberality toward us, was that he had gotten the full assents of two of as

sufficient experimented Masters as were any in his
fleet, by judgment of them that knew them, with
very sufficient gings to tary with me, and to em-
ploy themselves most earnestly in the action, as I
should appoint them, untill the terme which I
promised of our returne into England againe. The
names of one of those Masters was Abraham Kendall, the other Griffith Herne.

While these things were in hand, the provision
aforesaid being brought, and in bringing aboord,
my sayd Masters being also gone aboord, my sayd
barks having accepted of their charge, and mine
owne officers, with others in like sort of my company with them (all which was dispatched by the
sayd Generall the 12 of the sayde moneth) the 13
of the same there arose such an unwoonted storme,
and continued foure dayes, that had like to have
driven all on shore, if the Lord had not held his
holy hand over them, and the Generall very provi-
dently foreseene the woorst himselfe, then about
my dispatch putting himselfe aboord: but in the
end having driven sundry of the fleet to put to Sea
the *Francis* also with all my provisions, my two
Masters, and my company aboord, she was seene
to be free from the same, and to put cleere to Sea.

This storme having continued from the 13 to
the 16 of the moneth, and thus my barke put away
as aforesayd, the Generall comming ashore made
a new proffer unto me; which was a ship of 170
tunne, called The barke *Bonner,* with a sufficient
Master and guide to tary with me the time appointed, and victualled sufficiently to cary me and
my company into England, with all provisions as
before: but he tolde me that he would not for any
thing undertake to have her brought into our har-

bour, and therefore he was to leave her in the road, and to leave the care of the rest unto my selfe, and advised me to consider with my company of our case, and to deliver presently unto him in writing what I would require him to doe for us; which being within his power, he did assure me as well for his Captaines as for himselfe, shoulde be most willingly performed.

Heereupon calling such Captaines and gentlemen of my company as then were at hand, who were all as privy as my selfe to the Generals offer; their whole request was to me, that considering the case that we stood in, the weaknesse of our company, the small number of the same, the carying away of our first appointed barke, with those two speciall Masters, with our principall provisions in the same, by the very hand of God as it seemed, stretched out to take us from thence; considering also, that his second offer, though most honourable of his part, yet of ours not to be taken, insomuch as there was no possibility for her with any safety to be brought into the harbour: seeing furthermore, our hope for supply with Sir Richard Greenville, so undoubtedly promised us before Easter, not yet come, neither then likely to come this yeere, considering the doings in England for Flanders, and also for America, that therefore I would resolve my selfe with my company to goe into England in that fleet, and accordingly to make request to the Generall in all our names, that he would be pleased to give us present passage with him. Which request of ours by my selfe delivered unto him, hee most readily assented unto: and so he sending immediately his pinnesses unto our Island for the fetching away of a few that there were left with our baggage, the weather was so boisterous, and the pinnesses so often on ground, that the most of all we had, with all our Cards, Books and writings were by the Sailers cast overboard, the greater number of the fleet being much agrieved with their long and dangerous abode in that miserable road.

From whence the Generall in the name of the Almighty, weying his ankers (having bestowed us among his fleet) for the reliefe of whom hee had in that storme susteined more perill of wracke then in all his former most honourable actions against the Spanyards, with praises unto God for all, set saile the nineteenth of Iune 1596, and arrived in Portsmouth the seven and twentieth of Iuly the same yeere.

III

THE BIRTH OF VIRGINIA DARE[1]

(1587)

BY JOHN WHITE

The two and twentieth day of July we came safely to Cape Hatteras, where our ship and pinnace anchored. The Governor went aboard the pinnace accompanied by forty of his best men, intending to pass up to Roanoke. He hoped to

[1] Virginia Dare was the first child of English parentage born in America. Her father was Ananias Dare. She was named Virginia after the colony which had already received the name in compliment to Queen Elizabeth.

35

find those fifteen Englishmen whom Sir Richard Grenville had left there the year before. With these he meant to have a conference concerning the state of the country and the savages, intending then to return to the fleet and pass along the coast to the Bay of Chesapeake. Here we intended to make our settlement and fort according to the charge given us among other directions in writing under the hand of Sir Walter Raleigh. We passed to Roanoke and the same night at sunset went ashore on the island, in the place where our fifteen men were left. But we found none of them, nor any sign that they had been there, saving only that we found the bones of one of them, whom the savages had slain long before.

The Governor with several of his company walked the next day to the north end of the island, where Master Ralph Lane, with his men the year before, had built his fort with sundry dwelling houses. We hoped to find some signs here, or some certain knowledge of our fifteen men.

When we came thither we found the fort razed, but all the houses standing unhurt, saving that the lower rooms of them, and of the fort also, were overgrown with melons of different sorts, and deer were in rooms feeding on those melons. So we returned to our company without the hope of ever seeing any of the fifteen men living.

The same day an order was given that every man should be employed in remodelling those houses which we found standing, and in making more cottages.

On the eighteenth a daughter was born in Roanoke to Eleanor, the daughter of the Governor and the wife of Ananias Dare. This baby was christened on the Sunday following, and because this child was the first Christian born in Virginia she was named Virginia Dare.

By this time our shipmasters had unloaded the goods and victuals of the planters and taken wood and fresh water, and were newly calking and trimming their vessels for their return to England. The settlers also prepared their letters and news to send back to England.

BARTHOLOMEW GOSNOLD'S DIS-COVERY OF CAPE COD[1]

(1602)

I

BY GABRIEL ARCHER, ONE OF HIS COMPANIONS

The said captain [Gosnold] did set sail from Falmouth the day and year above written accompanied with thirty-two persons, whereof eight mariners and sailors, twelve purposing upon the discovery to return with the ship for England, the rest remain there for population. The fourteenth of April following, we had sight of Saint Mary's, an island of the Azores. . . .

The fifteenth day of May we had again sight of the land, which made ahead, being as we thought an island, by reason of a large sound that appeared westward between it and the main, for coming to the west end thereof, we did perceive a large opening, we called it Shoal Hope. Near this cape we

[1] Gosnold sailed from Falmouth, England, in 1602, Raleigh being interested in the expedition. He reached the New England coast in May of the same year, and discovered Cape Cod, to which, because of the abundance of codfish in neighboring waters he gave the name it bears. He afterward discovered Martha's Vineyard, and on the neighboring island of Cuttyhunk founded a settlement called Elizabeth, the first ever made in New England by Englishmen. This settlement lasted only a few weeks, the settlers returning to England.

came to anchor in fifteen fathoms, where we took great store of codfish, for which we altered the name, and called it Cape Cod. Here we saw sculls of herring, mackerel, and other small fish, in great abundance. This is a low sandy shoal, but without danger, also we came to anchor again in sixteen fathoms, fair by the land in the latitude of 42 degrees. This cape is well near a mile broad, and lieth north-east by east. The captain went here ashore and found the ground to be full of pease, strawberries, whortleberries, &c., as then unripe, the sand also by the shore somewhat deep, the firewood there by us taken in was of cypress, birch, witch-hazel and beech. A young Indian came here to the captain, armed with his bow and arrows, and had certain plates of copper hanging at his ears; he showed a willingness to help us in our occasions.

The sixteenth, we trended the coast southerly, which was all champaign and full of grass, but the island somewhat woody. Twelve leagues from Cape Cod, we descried a point with some breach, a good distance off, and keeping our luff to double it, we came on the sudden into shoal water, yet well quitted ourselves thereof. This breach we called Tucker's Terror, upon his exprest fear. The point we named Point Care; having passed

The entire group of islands, of which Cuttyhunk is one, are now known as the Elizabeth Islands. The township which these islands comprize bears Gosnold's name. Gosnold became active afterward in promoting the expedition which in 1607 resulted in the settlement of Jamestown. The report of the expedition to Cape Cod, from which this account is taken, is known as "The Relation of Captain Gosnold's Voyage." It was "delivered by Gabriel Archer, a gentleman in the said voyage." Archer's account is printed in "Old South Leaflets."

it we bore up again with the land, and in the night came with it anchoring in eight fathoms, the ground good.

The seventeenth, appeared many breaches round about us, so as we continued that day without remove. The eighteenth, being fair we sent forth the boat, to sound over a breach, that in our course lay of another point, by us called Gilbert's Point, who returned us four, five, six, and seven fathoms over. Also, a discovery of divers islands which after proved to be hills and hammocks, distinct within the land. This day there came unto the ship's side divers canoes, the Indians apparelled as aforesaid, with tobacco and pipes steeled with copper, skins, artificial strings and other trifles to barter; one had hanging about his neck a plate of rich copper, in length a foot, in breadth half a foot for a breastplate, the ears of all the rest had pendants of copper. Also, one of them had his face painted over, and head stuck with feathers in manner of a turkey-cock's train. These are more timorous than those of the Savage Rock, yet very thievish.

The nineteenth, we passed over the breach of Gilbert's Point in four or five fathoms, and anchored a league or somewhat more beyond it; between the last two points are two leagues, the interim, along shoal water, the latitude here is 41 degrees two third parts.

The twentieth, by the ship's side, we there killed penguins, and saw many sculls of fish. The coast from Gilbert's Point to the supposed isles lieth east and by south. Here also we discovered two inlets which might promise fresh water, inwardly whereof we perceived much smoke, as though some population had there been. This coast is very full of people, for that as we trended the same savages still run along the shore, as men much admiring at us.

The one-and-twentieth, we went coasting from Gilbert's Point to the supposed isles, in ten, nine, eight, seven, and six fathoms, close aboard the shore, and that depth lieth a league off. A little from the supposed isles, appeared unto us an opening, with which we stood, judging it to be the end of that which Captain Gosnold descried from Cape Cod, and as he thought to extend some thirty or more miles in length, and finding there but three fathoms a league off, we omitted to make further discovery of the same, calling it Shoal Hope.

From this opening the main lieth southwest, which coasting along we saw a disinhabited island, which so afterward appeared unto us: we bore with it, and named it Martha's Vineyard; from Shoal Hope it is eight leagues in circuit, the island is five miles, and hath 41 degrees and one quarter of latitude. The place most pleasant; for the two-and-twentieth, we went ashore, and found it full of wood, vines, gooseberry bushes, whortleberries, raspberries, eglantines, &c. Here we had cranes, stearnes, shoulers, geese, and divers other birds which there at that time upon the cliffs being sandy with some rocky stones, did breed and had young. In this place we saw deer: here we rode in eight fathoms near the shore where we took great store of cod,—as before at Cape Cod, but much better.

The three-and-twentieth we weighed, and toward night came to anchor at the northwest part of this island, where the next morning offered unto us fast running thirteen savages apparelled as aforesaid, and armed with bows and arrows without any fear. They brought tobacco, deer-skins, and some sodden fish. These offered themselves unto us in great familiarity, who seemed to be well-conditioned. They came more rich in copper than any before. This island is sound, and hath no danger about it.

The four-and-twentieth, we set sail and doubled the Cape of another island next unto it, which we called Dover Cliff, and then came into a fair sound[2], where we rode all night; the next morning we sent off one boat to discover another cape, that lay between us and the main, from which were a ledge of rocks a mile into the sea, but all above water, and without danger; we went about them, and came to anchor in eight fathoms, a quarter of a mile from the shore, in one of the stateliest sounds that ever I was in. This called we Gosnold's Hope; the north bank whereof is the main, which stretcheth east and west. This island Captain Gosnold called Elizabeth's isle, where we determined our abode; the distance between every one of these islands is, viz. from Martha's Vineyard to Dover Cliff, half a league over the sound, thence to Elizabeth's isle[3], one league distant. From Elizabeth's island unto the main is four leagues. On the north side, near adjoining unto the island Elizabeth, is an islet in compass half a

[2] Vineyard Sound.

[3] Now Cuttyhunk, the westermost of the chain of islands called the Elizabeth Islands, which separate Buzzards' Bay from Vineyard Sound.

mile, full of cedars, by me called Hill's Hap, to the northward of which, in the mouth of an opening on the main, appeareth another the like, that I called Hap's Hill, for that I hope much hap may be expected from it.

The eight-and-twentieth we entered counsel about our abode and plantation, which was concluded to be in the west part of Elizabeth's island. The north-east thereof running from out our ken. The south and north standeth in an equal parallel. . . .

The one-and-thirtieth, Captain Gosnold, desirous to see the main because of the distance, he set sail over; where coming to anchor, went ashore with certain of his company, and immediately there presented unto him men, kindness, women, and children, who, with all courteous kindness entertained him, giving him certain skins of wild beasts, which may be rich furs, tobacco, turtles, hemp, artificial strings colored, chains, and such like things as at the instant they had about them. These are a fair-conditioned people. On all the sea-coast along we found mussel shells that in color did represent mother-of-pearl, but not having means to dredge, could not apprehend further knowledge thereof. This main is the goodliest continent that ever we saw, promising more by far than we any way did expect; for it is replenished with fair fields, and in them fragrant flowers, also meadows, and hedged in with stately groves, being furnished also with pleasant brooks, and beautified with two main rivers that (as we judge) may haply become good harbors, and conduct us to the hopes men so greedily do thirst after. . . .

The first of June we employed ourselves in getting sassafras, and the building of our fort. The second, third, and fourth, we wrought hard to make ready our house for the provision to be had ashore to sustain us till our ship's return. This day from the main came to our ship's side a canoe, with their lord or chief commander, for that they made little stay only pointing to the sun, as in sign that the next day he would come and visit us, which he did accordingly.

The fifth, we continued our labor, when there came unto us ashore from the main fifty savages, stout and lusty men with their bows and arrows; amongst them there seemed to be one of authority, because the rest made an inclining respect unto him. The ship was at their coming a league off, and Captain Gosnold aboard, and so likewise Captain Gilbert, who almost never went ashore, the company with me only eight persons. These Indians in hasty manner came toward us, so as we thought fit to make a stand at an angle between the sea and a fresh water; I moved myself toward him seven or eight steps, and clapt my hands first on the sides of mine head, then on my breast, and after presented my musket with a threatening countenance, thereby to signify unto them, either a choice of peace or war, whereupon he using me with mine own signs of peace, I stept forth and embraced him; his company then all sat down in manner like greyhounds upon their heels, with whom my company fell a bartering. By this time Captain Gosnold was come with twelve men more from aboard, and to show the savage seignior that he was our Captain, we received him in a guard, which he passing through, saluted the seignior with ceremonies of our salutations, whereat he nothing moved or altered himself. Our Captain gave him

44

a straw hat and a pair of knives; the hat awhile he wore, but the knives he beheld with great marveling, being very bright and sharp; this our courtesy made them all in love with us. . . .

The eighth we divided the victuals, namely, the ship's store for England, and that of the planters, which by Captain Gilbert's allowance could be but six weeks for six months, whereby there fell out a controversy, the rather, for that some seemed secretly to understand of a purpose Captain Gilbert had not to return with supply of the issue, those goods should make by him to be carried home. Besides, there wanted not ambitious conceits in the minds of some wrangling and ill-disposed persons who overthrew the stay there at that time, which upon consultation thereof had, about five days after was fully resolved all for England again. There came in this interim aboard unto us, that stayed all night, an Indian, whom we used kindly, and the next day sent ashore; he showed himself the most sober of all the rest, we held him sent as a spy. In the morning, he filched away our pothooks, thinking he had not done any ill therein; being ashore we bid him strike fire, which with an emerald stone (such as the glaziers use to cut glass) he did. I take it to be the very same that in Latin is called *smiris*, for striking therewith upon touch-wood that of purpose he had, by means of a mineral stone used therein, sparkles proceeded and forthwith kindled with making of flame. The ninth, we continued working on our storehouse, for as yet remained in us a desired resolution of making stay. The tenth, Captain Gosnold fell down with the ship to the little islet of cedars, called Hill's Hap, to take in cedar wood, leaving me and nine more in the fort, only with three meals meat, upon promise to return the next day. . . .

The thirteenth, began some of our company that before vowed to stay, to make revolt: whereupon the planters diminishing, all was given over. The fourteenth, fifteenth and sixteenth, we spent in getting sassafras and fire-wood of cedar, leaving house and little fort, by ten men in nineteen days sufficient made to harbor twenty persons at least with their necessary provisions.

The seventeenth, we set sail, doubling the rocks of Elizabeth's island, and passing by Dover Cliff, came to anchor at Martha's Vineyard, being five leagues distant from our fort, where we went ashore, and had young cranes, herneshowes, and geese, which now were grown to pretty bigness.

The eighteenth, we set sail and bore for England, cutting off our shallop, that was well able to land five and twenty men or more, a boat very necessary for the like occasions. The winds do range most commonly upon this coast in the summer time, westerly. In our homeward course we observed the foresaid floating weeds to continue till we came within two hundred leagues of Europe. The three-and-twentieth of July we came to anchor before Exmouth.[4]

[4] From Exmouth the ship sailed for Portsmouth, her real destination.

II

GOSNOLD'S OWN ACCOUNT [1]

I was in good hope that my occasions would have allowed me so much liberty, as to have come unto you before this time; otherwise I would have written more at large concerning the country from whence we lately came, than I did: but not well remembering what I have already written (though I am assured that there is nothing set down disagreeing with the truth), I thought it fittest not to go about to add anything in writing, but rather to leave the report of the rest till I come myself; which now I hope shall be shortly, and so soon as with conveniency I may. In the mean time, notwithstanding whereas you seem not to be satisfied by that which I have already written, concerning some especial matters; I have here briefly (and as well as I can) added these few lines for your further satisfaction. . . .

We cannot gather, by anything we could observe in the people, or by any trial we had thereof ourselves, but that it is as healthful a climate as any can be. The inhabitants there, as I wrote before, being of tall stature, comely proportion, strong, active, and some of good years, and as it should seem very healthful, are sufficient proof of the healthfulness of the place. First, for ourselves (thanks be to God) we had not a man sick two days together in all our voyage; whereas others that went out with us, or about that time on other

[1] From a letter to his father, dated September 7, 1602.

47

voyages (especially such as went upon reprisal,) were most of them infected with sickness, whereof they lost some of their men, and brought home a many sick, returning notwithstanding long before us. But Verazzano, and others (as I take it, you may read in the Book of Discoveries), do more particularly entreat of the age of the people in that coast.

The sassafras which we brought we had upon the islands; where though we had little disturbance, and reasonable plenty; yet for that the greatest part of our people were employed about the fitting of our house, and such like affairs, and a few (and those but easy laborers) undertook this work, the rather because we were informed before our going forth, that a ton was sufficient to cloy England, and further, for that we had resolved upon our return, and taken view of our victual, we judged it then needful to use expedition; which afterward we had more certain proof of; for when we came to an anchor before Portsmouth, which was some four days after we made the land, we had not one cake of bread, nor any drink, but a little vinegar left: for these and other reasons we returned no otherwise laden than you have heard. And thus much I hope shall suffice till I can myself come to give you further notice, which though it be not so soon as I could have wished, yet I hope it shall be in convenient time.

THE FOUNDING OF JAMESTOWN

(1607)

I

BY CAPTAIN JOHN SMITH[1]

Captaine Bartholomew Gosnoll, one of the first movers of this plantation, having many yeares solicited many of his friends, but found small assistants; at last prevailed with some Gentlemen, as Captaine Iohn Smith, Master Edward-maria Wingfield, Master Robert Hunt, and divers others, who depended a yeare vpon his proiects, but nothing could be effected, till by their great charge and industrie, it came to be apprehended by certaine of the Nobilitie, Gentry, and Marchants, so that his Maiestie by his letters patents, gaue commission for establishing Councels, to direct here; and to gouerne, and to execute there. To effect this, was spent another yeare, and by that, three ships were provided, one of 100 Tuns, another of 40, and a

[1] From Smith's "General History of Virginia." Edward Arber has contended that, had not John Smith "strove, fought and endured as he did the present United States of America might never have come into existence." Spaniards and French alike had failed in their attempts at colonization, and so had the repeated expeditions sent out by Sir Walter Raleigh. Smith carried the Jamestown settlement through its difficulties,—Smith, the "self-denying, energetic, so full of resources, and so trained in dealing with the savage races." Had Jamestown failed the Pilgrim fathers "would not have gone to New England." Smith was not the sole author of the "History of Virginia." Others contributed to the work.

Pinnace of 20. The transportation of the company was committed to Captaine Christopher Newport, a Marriner well practised for the Westerne parts of America. But their orders for government were put in a box, not to be opened, nor the governours knowne vntill they arrived in Virginia. . . . On the 19 of December, 1606, we set sayle from Blackwell, but by vnprosperous winds, were kept six weekes in the sight of England; all which time, Master Hunt our Preacher, was so weake and sicke, that few expected his recovery.

We watered at the Canaries, we traded with the Salvages at Dominica; three weekes we spent in refreshing our selues amongst these west-India Isles; in Gwardalupa we found a bath so hot, as in it we boyled Porck as well as over the fire. And a little Isle called Monica, we tooke from the bushes with our hands, neare two hogsheads full of Birds in three or foure houres. In Mevis, Mona, and the Virgin Isles, we spent some time; where, with a lothsome beast like a Crocodil, called a Gwayn, Tortoises, Pellicans, Parrots, and fishes, we daily feasted.

Gone from thence in search of Virginia, the company was not a little discomforted, seeing the Marriners had 3 dayes passed their reckoning and found no land; so that Captaine Ratliffe (Captaine of the Pinnace) rather desired to beare vp the helme to returne for England, then make further search. But God the guider of all good actions, forcing them by an extreame storme to hull all night, did driue them by his providence to their desired Port, beyond all their expectations; for never any of them had seene that coast.

The first land they made they called Cape Henry; where thirtie of them recreating themselues on shore, were assaulted by fiue Salvages, who hurt two of the English very dangerously.

That night was the box opened, and the orders read, in which Bartholomew Gosnoll, Iohn Smith, Edward Wingfield, Christopher Newport, Iohn Ratliffe, Iohn Martin, and George Kendall, were named to be the Councell, and to choose a President amongst them for a year, who with the Councell should governe. Matters of moment were to be examined by a Iury, but determined by the maior part of the Councell, in which the President had two voyces.

Untill the 13 of May they sought a place to plant in; then the Councell was sworne, Master Wingfield was chosen President, and an Oration made, why Captain Smith was not admitted of the Councell as the rest.

Now falleth every man to worke, the Councell contrive the Fort, the rest cut downe trees to make place to pitch their Tents; some provide clapbord to relade the ships, some make gardens, some nets, &c. The Salvages often visited vs kindly. The Presidents overweening iealousie would admit no exercise at armes, or fortification but the boughs of trees cast together in the forme of a halfe moone by the extraordinary paines and diligence of Captaine Kendall.

Newport, Smith, and twentie others, were sent to discover the head of the river: by divers small habitations they passed, in six dayes they arrived at a Towne called Powhatan, consisting of some twelue houses, pleasantly seated on a hill; before it three fertile Iles, about it many of their cornefields, the place is very pleasant, and strong by nature, of this place the Prince is called Powhatan, and his people Powhatans. To this place the river is navigable: but higher within a myle, by reason of the Rocks and Isles, there is not passage for a small Boat, this they call the Falles[1]. The people in all parts kindly intreated them, till being returned within twentie myles of Iames towne, they gaue iust cause of iealousie: but had God not blessed the discoverers otherwise than those at the Fort, there had then beene an end of that plantation; for at the Fort, where they arrived the next day, they found 17 men hurt, and a boy slaine by the Salvages, and had it not chanced a crosse barre shot from the Ships strooke downe a bough from a tree amongst them, that caused them to retire, our men had all beene slaine, being securely all at worke, and their armes in dry fats.

Herevpon the President was contented the Fort should be pallisadoed, the Ordnance mounted, his men armed and exercised: for many were the assaults, and ambuscadoes of the Salvages, and our men by their disorderly stragling were often hurt, when the Salvages by the nimblenesse of their heels well escaped.

What toyle we had, with so small a power to guard our workemen adayes, watch all night, resist our enemies, and effect our businesse, to relade the ships, cut downe trees, and prepare the ground to plant our Corne, &c. I referre to the Readers consideration. Six weekes being spent in this manner, Captaine Newport (who was hired onely for our transportation) was to returne with the ships. . .

[1] Richmond.

Being thus left to our fortunes, it fortuned that within ten days scarce ten amongst vs could either goe, or well stand, such extreame weaknes and sicknes oppressed vs. And thereat none need marvaile, if they consider the cause and reason, which was this.

Whilst the ships stayed, our allowance was somewhat bettered, by a daily proportion of Bisket, which the sailers would pilfer to sell, giue, or exchange with vs, for money, Saxefras, furres, or loue. But when they departed, there remained neither taverne, beere house, nor place of reliefe, but the common Kettell. Had we beene as free from all sinnes as gluttony, and drunkennesse, we might haue beene canonized for Saints; But our President would never haue beene admitted, for ingrossing to his private, Oatmeale, Sacke, Oyle, *Aquavitæ*, Beefe, Egges, or what not, but the Kettell; that indeed he allowed equally to be distributed, and that was halfe a pint of wheat, and as much barley boyled with water for a man a day, and this having fryed some 6 weekes in the ships hold, contained as many wormes as graines; so that we might truely call it rather so much bran than corne, our drinke was water, our lodgings Castles in the ayre.

With this lodging and dyet, our extreame toile in bearing and planting Pallisadoes, so strained and bruised vs, and our continuall labour in the extremitie of the heat had so weakened vs, as were cause sufficient to haue made vs as miserable in our natiue Countrey, or any other place in the world.

From May, to September, those that escaped, liued vpon Sturgeon, and Sea-crabs, fiftie in this time we buried, the rest seeing the Presidents projects to escape these miseries in our Pinnace by flight (who all this time had neither felt want nor sicknes) so moved our dead spirits, as we deposed him; and established Ratcliffe in his place, (Gosnoll being dead) Kendall deposed. Smith newly recovered, Martin and Ratcliffe was by his care preserved and relieued, and the most of the souldiers recovered with the skilfull diligence of Master Thomas Wotton our Chirurgian generall.

But now was all our provision spent, the Sturgeon gone, all helps abandoned, each houre expecting the fury of the Salvages; when God the patron of all good indevours, in that desperate extremitie so changed the hearts of the Salvages, that they brought such plenty of their fruits, and provision, as no man wanted. . . .

The new President, and Martin, being little beloved, of weake iudgement in dangers, and lesse industrie in peace, committed the managing of all things abroad to Captaine Smith: who by his owne example, good words, and faire promises, set some to mow, others to binde thatch, some to build houses, others to thatch them, himselfe alwayes bearing the greatest taske for his owne share, so that in short time, he provided most of them lodgings, neglecting any for himselfe.

This done, seeing the Salvages superfluitie beginne to decrease (with some of his workmen) shipped himselfe in the Shallop to search the Country for trade. The want of the language, knowledge to mannage his boat without sailes, the want of a sufficient power (knowing the multitude of the Salvages), apparell for his men, and other necessaries, were infinite impediments.

Being but six or seauen in company he went
downe the river to Kecoughtan: where at first
they scorned him, as a famished man; and would
in derision offer him a handfull of Corne, a peece
of bread, for their swords and muskets, and such
like proportions also for their apparell. But seeing by trade and courtesie there was nothing to
be had, he made bold to try such conclusions as
necessitie inforced, though contrary to his Commission: Let fly his muskets, ran his boat on shore;
whereat they all fled into the woods.

So marching towards their houses, they might
see great heapes of corne: much adoe he had to
restraine his hungry souldiers from present taking
of it, expecting as it hapned that the Salvages
would assault them, as not long after they did
with a most hydeous noyse. Sixtie or seauentie
of them, some blacke, some red, some white, some
party-coloured, came in a square order, singing
and dauncing out of the woods, with their Okee
(which was an Idoll made of skinnes, stuffed with
mosse, all painted and hung with chaines and copper) borne before them: and in this manner, being
well armed with Clubs, Targets, Bowes and Arrowes, they charged the English, that so kindly
receiued them with their muskets loaden with Pis-
toll shot, that downe fell their God, and divers lay
sprauling on the ground; the rest fled againe to
the woods, and ere long sent one of their Qui-
youghkasoucks to offer peace, and redeeme their
Okee.

Smith told them, if onely six of them would
come vnarmed and loade his boat, he would not
only be their friend, but restore them their Okee,
and giue them Beads, Copper, and Hatchets be-

sides: which on both sides was to their contents performed: and then they brought him Venison, Turkies, wild foule, bread, and what they had; singing and dauncing in signe of friendship till they departed.

In his returne he discovered the Towne and Country of Warraskoyack.

> Thus God vnboundlesse by his power,
> Made them thus kind, would vs deuour.

Smith perceiving (notwithstanding their late miserie) not any regarded but from hand to mouth: (the company being well recovered) caused the Pinnace to be provided with things fitting to get provision for the yeare following; but in the interim he made 3, or 4, iournies and discovered the people of Chickahamania: yet what he carefully provided the rest carelesly spent.

Wingfield and Kendall liuing in disgrace, seeing all things at randome in the absence of Smith, the companies dislike of their Presidents weaknes, and their small loue to Martins never mending sicknes, strengthened themselues with the sailers and other confederates, to regaine their former credit and authority, or at least such meanes abord the Pinnace, (being fitted to saile as Smith had oppointed for trade) to alter her course and to goe for England.

Smith vnexpectedly returning had the plot discovered to him, much trouble he had to prevent it, till with store of sakre and musket shot he forced them stay or sinke in the riuer: which action cost the life of captaine Kendall.

These brawles are so disgustful, as some will

say they were better forgotten, yet all men of good iudgement will conclude it were better their basenes should be manifest to the world, then the busines beare the scorne and shame of their excused disorders.

The President and captaine Archer not long after intended also to haue abandoned the country, which project also was curbed, and suppressed by Smith. The Spaniard never more greedily desired gold than he victuall; nor his souldiers more to abandon the Country, then he to keepe it. But finding plentie of Corne in the riuer of Chickahamania, where hundreds of Salvages in diuers places stood with baskets expecting his comming.

And now the winter approaching, the rivers became so covered with swans, geese, duckes, and cranes, that we daily feasted with good bread. Virginia pease, pumpions, and putchamins, fish, fowle, and diverse sorts of wild beasts as fat as we could eate them: so that none of our Tuftaffaty humorists desired to goe for England.

But our Comœdies never endured long without a Tragedie; some idle exceptions being muttered against Captaine Smith, for not discovering the head of Chickahamania river, and taxed by the Councell, to be slow in so worthy an attempt. The next voyage hee proceeded so farre that with much labour by cutting of trees insunder he made his passage; but when his Barge could passe no farther, he left her in a broad bay out of danger of shot, commanding none should goe a shore till his returne; himselfe with two English and two Salvages went vp higher in a Canowe; but hee was not long absent, but his men went a shore, whose want of government gaue both occasion and opportunity to the Salvages to surprise one George Cassen, whom they slew, and much failed not to have cut of the boat and all the rest.

Smith, little dreaming of that accident, being got to the marshes at the rivers head, twentie myles in the desert, had his two men slaine (as is supposed) sleping by the Canowe, whilst himselfe by fowling sought them victuall: who finding he was beset with 200 Salvages, two of them hee slew still defending himselfe with the ayd of a Salvage his guid, whom he bound to his arme with his garters, and vsed him as a buckler, yet he was shot in his thikh a little, and had many arrowes that stucke in his cloathes but no great hurt, till at last they tooke him prisoner.

When this newes came to Iames towne, much was their sorrow for his losse, fewe expecting what ensued. Sixe or seuen weekes those Barbarians kept him prisoner, many strange triumphes and coniurations they made of him, yet hee so demeaned himselfe amongst them, as he not onely diverted them from surprising the Fort, but procured his owne libertie, and got himselfe and his company such estimation amongst them, that those Salvages admired him more than their owne Quiyouckosucks.

At last they brought him to Meronocomoco, where was Powhatan their Emperor. Here more than two hundred of those grim Courtiers stood wondering at him, as he had beene a monster; till Powhatan and his trayne had put themselues in their greatest braveries. Before a fire vpon a seat like a bedsted, he sat covered with a great robe, made of Rarowcun skinnes, and all the tayles hanging by. On either hand did sit a young wench

of 15 or 18 yeares, and along on each side the
house, two rowes of men, and behind them as many
women, with all their heads and shoulders painted
red: many of their heads bedecked with the white
downe of Birds; but every one with something:
and a great chayne of white beads about their
necks.

At his entrance before the king, all the people
gaue a great shout. The Queene of Appamatuck
was appointed to bring him water to wash his
hands, and another brought him a bunch of
feathers, in stead of a Towell to ry them: having
feasted him after their best barbarous manner
they could, a long consultation was held, but the
conclusion was, two great stones were brought before Powhatan; then as many as could layd hands
on him, dragged him to them, and thereon laid his
head, and being ready with their clubs, to beate
out his braines, Pocohontas, the King's dearest
daughter, when no intreaty could prevaile, got his
head in her armes, and laide her owne vpon his
to saue him from death: whereat the Emperour
was contented he should liue to make him hatchets,
and her bells, beads, and copper; for they thought
him aswell of all occupations as themselues. For
the King himselfe will make his owne robes, shooes,
bowes, arrowes, pots; plant, hunt, or doe any
thing so well as the rest.

> They say he bore a pleasant shew,
> But sure his heart was sad.
> For who can pleasant be, and rest,
> That lives in feare and dreade:
> And having life suspected, doth
> It still suspected lead.

Two dayes after, Powhatan having disguised himselfe in the most fearefullest manner he could, caused Captain Smith to be brought forth to a great house in the woods, and there vpon a mat by the fire to be left alone. Not long after from behinde a mat that divided the house, was made the most dolefullest noyse he ever heard; then Powhatan more like a devill than a man, with some two hundred more as blacke as himselfe, came vnto him and told him now they were friends, and presently he should goe to Iames towne, to send him two great gunnes, and a gryndstone, for which he would giue him the Country of Capahowosick, and for ever esteeme him as his sonne Nantaquoud.

So to Iames towne with 12 guides Powhatan sent him. That night they quartered in the woods, he still expecting (as he had done all this long time of his imprisonment) every houre to be put to one death or other: for all their feasting. But almightie God (by his divine providence) had mollified the hearts of those sterne Barbarians with compassion. The next morning betimes they came to the Fort, where Smith having vsed the Salvages with what kindnesse he could, he shewed Rawhunt, Powhatans trusty servant, two demi-Culverings and a millstone to carry Powhatan: they found them somewhat too heavie; but when they did see him discharge them, being loaded with stones, among the boughs of a great tree loaded with Isickles the yce and branches came so tumbling downe, that the poore Salvages ran away halfe dead with feare. But at last we regained some conference with them, and gaue them such toyes; and sent to Powhatan, his women, and children such presents, as gaue them in generall full content.

Now in Iames Towne they were all in combustion, the strongest preparing once more to run away with the Pinnace; which with the hazzard of his life, with Sakre falcon and musket shot, Smith forced now the third time to stay or sinke.

Some no better than they should be, had plotted with the President, the next day to haue put him to death by the Leviticall law, for the liues of Robinson and Emry; pretending the fault was his that had led them to their ends; but he quickly tooke such order with such Lawyers, that he layd them by the heeles till he sent some of them prisoners for England.

Now ever once in foure or fiue dayes, Pocahontas with her attendants, brought him so much provision, that saved many of their liues, that els for all this had starved with hunger. . . .

Thus you may see what difficulties still crossed any good indevour; and the good successe of the businesse being thus oft brought to the very period of destruction; yet you see by what strange means God hath still delivered it.

Now whether it had beene better for Captaine Smith, to haue concluded with any of those severall proiects, to haue abandoned the Countrey, with some ten or twelue of them, who were called the better sort, and haue left Master Hunt our Preacher, Master Anthony Gosnoll, a most honest, worthy, and industrious Gentleman, Master Thomas Wotton and some 27 others of his Countrymen to the fury of the Salvages, famine, and all manner of mischiefes, and inconveniences, (for they were but fortie in all to keepe possession of this large

Country;) or starue himselfe with them for company, for want of lodging: or but adventuring abroad to make them provision, or by his opposition to preserve the action, and saue all their liues; I leaue to the censure of all honest men to consider.

THE FIRST AMERICAN LEGISLA-
TIVE ASSEMBLY

(1619)

BY JOHN TWINE, ITS SECRETARY[1]

A reporte of the manner of proceedings in the
General assembly convented at James citty in Virginia, July 30, 1619, consisting of the Gouverno^r,
the Counsell of Estate and two Burgesses elected
out of eache Incorporation and Plantation, and
being dissolved the 4th of August next ensuing.

First. Sir George Yeardley, Knight Governo^r
& Captaine general of Virginia, sente his sumons
all over the Country, as well to invite those of the
Counsell of Estate that were absente as also for
the election of Burgesses. . . .

The most convenient place we could finde to sitt
in was the Quire of the Churche Where Sir George
Yeardley, the Governour, being sett down in his
accustomed place, those of the Counsel of Estate
sate nexte him on both handes, excepte onely the
Secretary then appointed Speaker, who sate right
before him, John Twine, clerke of the General
assembly, being placed nexte the Speaker, and
Thomas Pierse, the Sergeant, standing at the
barre, to be ready for any Service the Assembly

[1] This account is taken from the official report of the as-
sembly, of which Twine was clerk. It is printed in the
"Colonial Records of Virginia," and in Hart's "American
History Told by Contemporaries."

should comaund him. But forasmuch as men's affaires doe little prosper where God's service is neglected, all the Burgesses tooke their places in the Quire till a prayer was said by Mr. Bucke, the Minister, that it would please God to guide and sanctifie all our proceedings to his owne glory and the good of this Plantation. Prayer being ended, to the intente that as we had begun at God Almighty, so we might proceed wth awful and due respecte towards the Lieutenant, our most gratious and dread Soveraigne, all the Burgesses were intreatted to retyre themselves into the body of the Churche, wch being done, before they were fully admitted, they were called in order and by name, and so every man (none staggering at it) tooke the oathe of Supremacy, and then entred the Assembly. . . .

These obstacles removed, the Speaker, who a long time had bene extreame sickly and therefore not able to passe through long harrangues, delivered in briefe to the whole assembly the occasions of their meeting. Which done, he read unto them the comission for establishing the Counsell of Estate and the general Assembly, wherein their duties were described to the life.

Having thus prepared them, he read over unto them the greate Charter, or comission of priviledges, orders and lawes, sent by Sir George Yeardly out of Englande. Which for the more ease of the Committies, having divided into fower books, he read the former two the same forenoon for expeditious sake, a second time over and so they were referred to the perusall of twoe Comitties, wch did reciprocally consider of either, and accordingly brought in their opinions. But some

men may here objecte to what ende we should presume to referre that to the examination of the
Comitties wch the Counsell and Company in Eng-
gland had already resolved to be perfect, and did
expecte nothing but our assente thereunto? To
this we answere that we did it not to the ende to
correcte or controll anything therein contained,
but onely in case we should finde ought not per-
fectly squaring wth the state of this Colony or any
lawe wch did presse or binde too harde, that we
might by waye of humble petition, .seeke to have
it redressed, especially because this great Charter
is to binde us and our heyers for ever. . . .

After dinner the Governo^r and those that were
not of the Comitties sate a seconde time, while the
said Comitties were employed in the perusall of
those twoe bookes. And whereas the Speaker had
propounded fower severall objects for the Assembly to consider on: namely, first, the great charter
of orders, lawes, and priviledges; Secondly, which
of the instructions given by the Counsel in England to my lo: la: warre, Captain Argall or Sir
George Yeardley, might conveniently putt on the
habite of lawes; Thirdly, what lawes might issue
out of the private conceipte of any of the Burgesses, or any other of the Colony; and lastly,
what petitions were fitt to be sente home for England. It pleased the Governou^r for expedition
sake to have the second objecte of the fower to be
examined & prepared by himselfe and the Non-
Comitties. Wherein after having spente some
three howers conference, the twoe Committies
brought in their opinions concerning the twoe
former bookes, (the second of which beginneth at
these words of the Charter: And forasmuche as

our intente is to establish one equall and uniforme
kinde of government over all Virginia &c.,) w^ch
the whole Assembly, because it was late, deffered
to treatt of till the next morning. . . .

There remaining no farther scruple in the mindes
of the Assembly, touching the said great Charter
of lawes, orders and priviledges, the Speaker putt
the same to the question, and so it had both the
general assent and the applause of the whole assembly, who, as they professed themselves in the
first place most submissivily thankfull to almighty
god, therefore so they commaunded the Speaker
to returne (as nowe he doth) their due and humble
thankes to the Treasurer, Counsell and company
for so many priviledges and favours as well in
their owne names as in the names of the whole
Colony whom they represented.

This being dispatched we fell once more debating
of suche instructions given by the Counsell in
England to several Governo^rs as might be con-
verted into lawes, the last whereof was the Establishment of the price of Tobacco, namely, of the
best at 3d and the second at 18d the pounde, . . .

Here begin the lawes drawen out of the Instructions given by his Mat^ies Counsell of Virginia in
England to my lo: la warre, Captain Argall and
Sir George Yeardley, knight. By this present Generall Assembly be it enacted, that no injury or
oppression be wrought by the Englishe against
the Indians whereby the present peace might be
disturbed and antient quarrells might be revived.
And farther be it ordained that the Chicohomini
are not to be excepted out of this lawe; untill
either that suche order come out of Englande, or
that they doe provoke us by some newe injury.

Against Idleness, Gaming, durunkeness & excesse in apparell the Assembly hath enacted as followeth:

First, in detestation of Idlenes be it enacted, that if any men be founde to live as an Idler or renagate, though a freedman, it shalbe lawfull for that Incorporation or Plantation to wch he belongeth to appoint him a M^r to serve for wages, till he shewe apparent signes of amendment.

Against gaming at dice & Cardes be it ordained by this present assembly that the winner or winners shall lose all his or their winninges and both winners and loosers shall forfaicte ten shillings a man, one ten shillings whereof to go to the discoverer, and the rest to charitable & pious uses in the Incorporation where the faulte is comitted.

Against drunkenness be it also decreed that if any private person be found culpable thereof, for the first time he is to be reprooved privately by the Minister, the second time publiquely, the thirde time to lye in boltes 12 howers in the house of the Provost Marshall & to paye his fee, and if he still continue in that vice, to undergo suche severe punishment as the Governo^r and Counsell of Estate shall thinke fitt to be inflicted on him. But if any officer offende in this crime, the first time he shall receive a reprooff from the Governour, the second time he shall openly be reprooved in the churche by the minister, and the third time he shall first be comitted and then degraded. Provided it be understood that the Governo^r hath always power to restore him when he shall, in his discretion thinke fitte.

Against excesse in apparell that every man be cessed in the churche for all publique contributions, if he be unmarried according to his owne apparrell, if he be married according to his owne and his wives, or either of their apparrell. . . .

Be it enacted by this present assembly that for laying a surer foundation of the conversion of the Indians to Christian Religion, eache towne, citty, Borrough, and particular plantation do obtaine unto themselves by just means a certaine number of the natives' children to be educated by them in the true religion and civile course of life—of wch children the most towardly boyes in witt & graces of nature to be brought up by them in the first elements of litterature, so to be fitted for the Colledge intended for them that from thence they may be sente to that worke of conversion.

As touching the business of planting corne this present Assembly doth ordaine that yeare by yeare all & every householder and householders have in store for every servant he or they shall keep, and also for his or their owne persons, whether they have any Servants or no, one spare barrell of corne, to be delivered out yearly, either upon sale or exchange as need shall require. For the neglecte of wch duty he shalbe subject to the censure of the Govern^r and Counsell of Estate. Provided always that the first yeare of every newe man this lawe shall not be of force. . . .

All ministers shall duely read divine service, and exercise their ministerial function according to the Ecclesiastical lawes and orders of the churche of Englande, and every Sunday in the afternoon shall Catechize suche as are not yet ripe to come to the Com. And whosoever shalbe found negligent or faulty in this kinde shalbe subject to the censure of the Governo^r and Counsell.

All persons whatsoever upon the Sabaoth daye shall frequente divine service and sermons both forenoon and afternoon, and all suche as beare arms shall bring their pieces, swordes, poulder and shotte. And every one that shall transgresse this lawe shall forfaicte three shillings a time to the ues of the churche, all lawful and necessary impediments excepted. But if a servant in this case shall wilfully neglecte his M^{rs} commande he shall suffer bodily punishmente.

No maide or woman servant, either now resident in the Colonie or hereafter to come, shall contract herselfe in marriage wthout either the consente of her parents, or of her M^r or M^{ris}, or of the magistrat and minister of the place both together. And whatsoever minister shall marry or contracte any suche persons wthout some of the foresaid consentes shalbe subjecte to the severe censure of the Govern^r and Counsell of Estate. . .

In sume Sir George Yeardley, the Governo^r prorogued the said General Assembly till the firste of Marche, which is to fall out this present yeare of 1619, and in the mean season dissolved the same.

THE ORIGIN OF NEGRO SLAVERY IN AMERICA

I

IN THE WEST INDIES

(1518)

BY SIR ARTHUR HELPS[1]

The outline of Las Casas'[2] scheme was as follows: The King was to give to every laborer willing to emigrate to Española his living during the journey from his place of abode to Seville, at the rate of half a real a day throughout the journey, for great and small, child and parent. At Seville the emigrants were to be lodged in the Casa de la Contratacion (the India House), and were to have from eleven to thirteen maravedis a day. From thence they were to have a free passage to Española, and to be provided with food for a year. And if the climate "should try them so much" that at the expiration of this year they should not be able

---

[1] Helps was an English writer who is best known for his social essays entitled "Friends in Council." He was the author of several works on America, including "The Spanish Conquest in America."

[2] Las Casas was a Dominican, born in Spain, who came to the West Indies in 1502 and devoted himself to protecting the Indians against slavery at the hands of their conquerors. In 1544 he was made a Mexican bishop.

to work for themselves, the King was to continue to maintain them; but this extra maintenance was to be put down to the account of the emigrants, as a loan which they were to repay. The King was to give them lands—his own lands—furnish them with plowshares and spades, and provide medicines for them. Lastly, whatever rights and profits accrued from their holdings were to become hereditary. This was certainly a most liberal plan of emigration. And, in addition, there were other privileges held out as inducements to these laborers.

In connection with the above scheme, Las Casas, unfortunately for his reputation in after-ages, added another provision, namely, that each Spanish resident in the island should have license to import a dozen negro slaves. The origin of this suggestion was, as he informs us, that the colonists had told him that, if license were given them to import a dozen negro slaves each, they, the colonists, would then set free the Indians. And so, recollecting that statement of the colonists, he added this provision. Las Casas, writing his history in his old age, thus frankly owns his error:

"This advice, that license should be given to bring negro slaves to these lands, the *clerigo* Casas first gave, not considering the injustice with which the Portuguese take them and make them slaves; which advice, after he had apprehended the nature of the thing, he would not have given for all he had in the world. For he always held that they had been made slaves unjustly and tyrannically; for the same reason holds good of them as of the Indians."

The above confession is delicately and truthfully worded—"not considering"; he does not say, not being aware of; but though it was a matter known to him, his moral sense was not watchful, as it were, about it. We must be careful not to press the admissions of a generous mind too far, or to exaggerate the importance of the suggestion of Las Casas. It would be quite erroneous to look upon this suggestion as being the introduction of negro slavery. From the earliest times of the discovery of America, negroes had been sent there. But what is of more significance, and what it is strange that Las Casas was not aware of, or did not mention, the Hieronymite Fathers had also come to the conclusion that negroes must be introduced into the West Indies. Writing in January, 1518, when the fathers could not have known what was passing in Spain in relation to this subject, they recommended licenses to be given to the inhabitants of Española, or to other persons, to bring negroes there. From the tenor of their letter it appears that they had before recommended the same thing. Zuazo, the judge of residencia, and the legal colleague of Las Casas, wrote to the same effect. He, however, suggested that the negroes should be placed in settlements and married. Fray. Bernardino de Manzanedo, the Hieronymite father, sent over to counteract Las Casas, gave the same advice as his brethren about the introduction of negroes. He added a proviso, which does not appear in their letter—perhaps it did exist in one of the earlier ones—that there should be as many women as men sent over, or more.

The suggestion of Las Casas was approved of by the Chancellor; and, indeed, it is probable there was hardly a man of that time who would have seen further than the excellent clerigo did. Las Casas was asked what number of negroes would suffice? He replied that he did not know; upon which a letter was sent to the officers of the India House at Seville to ascertain the fit number in their opinion. They said that four thousand at present would suffice, being one thousand for each of the islands, Española, Porto Rico, Cuba, and Jamaica. Somebody now suggested to the Governor, De Bresa, a Fleming of much influence and a member of the council, that he should ask for this license to be given to him. De Bresa accordingly asked the King for it, who granted his request; and the Fleming sold this license to certain Genoese merchants for twenty-five thousand ducats, having obtained from the King a pledge that for eight years he should give no other license of this kind.

The consequence of this monopoly enjoyed by the Genoese merchants was that negroes were sold at a great price, of which there are frequent complaints. Both Las Casas and Pasamonte—rarely found in accord—suggested to the King that it would be better to pay the twenty-five thousand ducats and resume the license, or to abridge its term. Figueroa, writing to the Emperor from Sonto Domingo, says: "Negroes are very much in request; none have come for about a year. It would have been better to have given De Bresa the customs duties—*i.e.*, the duties that had been usually paid on the importation of slaves—than to have placed a prohibition." I have scarcely a doubt that the immediate effect of the measure adopted in consequence of the clerigo's suggestion was greatly to check that importation of negro slaves which otherwise, had the license been general, would have been very abundant.

Before quitting this part of the subject, something must be said for Las Casas which he does not allege for himself. This suggestion of his about the negroes was not an isolated one. Had all his suggestions been carried out, and the Indians thereby been preserved, as I firmly believe they might have been, these negroes might have remained a very insignificant number in the general population. By the destruction of Indians a void in the laborious part of the community was being constantly created, which had to be filled up by the labor of negroes. The negroes could bear the labor in the mines much better than the Indians; and any man who perceived that a race, of whose Christian virtues and capabilities he thought highly, were fading away by reason of being subjected to labor which their natures were incompetent to endure, and which they were most unjustly condemned to, might prefer the misery of the smaller number of another race treated with equal injustice, but more capable of enduring it. I do not say that Las Casas considered all these things; but, at any rate, in estimating his conduct, we must recollect that we look at the matter centuries after it occurred, and see all the extent of the evil arising from circumstances which no man could then be expected to foresee, and which were inconsistent with the rest of the clerigo's plans for the preservation of the Indians.

I suspect that the wisest among us would very likely have erred with him; and I am not sure that, taking all his plans together, and taking for granted, as he did then, that his influence at court was to last, his suggestion about the negroes was an impolite one.

II

ITS BEGINNINGS IN THE UNITED STATES

(1620)

BY JOHN A. DOYLE [1]

The economical success which had attended the introduction of negroes into the West Indies made it almost certain that the American colonies would betake themselves to the same resource. The first introduction of negroes is commonly placed in the year 1620, when a Dutch ship landed twenty of them for sale at Jamestown. For some years their numbers increased but slowly. In 1649 Virginia contained only three hundred. By 1661 they had increased to two thousand, while the indented servants were four times that number. Twenty-two years later, if we may trust Culpepper's statement, the number of white servants was nearly doubled, while that of the negroes had only increased by one-half. Of their numbers and proportions in Maryland and North Carolina we have no definite evidence. In South Carolina negro slavery seems to have been almost from the outset the prevalent form of industry.

[1] From Doyle's "English Colonies in America." By permission of the publishers, Henry Holt & Co.

As early as 1708 we are told that three-fifths of the population were blacks. This alteration in the relative numbers of white servants and black slaves was accelerated by a change which had come over the commercial policy of the English Government. In 1662 the Royal African Company was incorporated. At the head of it was the Duke of York, and the King himself was a large shareholder. The chief profit of this company was derived from the exportation of negroes from Guinea to the plantations. The King and his brother henceforth had a direct interest in limiting the supply of indented servants, and it is not unlikely that this explains why Jeffreys for once deviated into the paths of humanity and justice. . . .

Had negro slavery never existed, had the natural resources of the Southern colonies favored the growth of a free yeomanry, the system of indenture would have been admirably fitted to establish a population of small proprietors, trained in habits of industry and in a competent knowledge of agriculture. The social and industrial life of the colonies forbade this. A peasant proprietary can only exist under severe restraints as to increase, or where there is urban life to take off the surplus population for trades and handicrafts. The Southern colonies fulfilled neither of these conditions. When the servant was out of his indentures there was no place for him. He could not become a shopkeeper or craftsman or a free agricultural laborer, for none of these callings existed. Moreover, the very same conditions of soil and climate which enabled slavery to exist, made it possible for the freeman to procure a scanty livelihood, without any habits of settled industry.

Thus the liberated servant became an idler, socially corrupt, and often politically dangerous. He furnished that class justly described by a Virginian of that day as "a foeculum of beings called overseers, a most abject, unprincipled race." He was the forerunner, and possibly in some degree the progenitor, of that class who did so much to intensify the evils of slavery, the "mean whites" of later times. . . .

When once negro slavery was firmly established, any rival form of industry was doomed. For it is an economical law of slavery, that where it exists it must exist without a rival. It can only succeed where it is a predominant form of labor. The utility of the slave is that of a machine. When once he has been trained to any special kind of industry, no attempts to enlarge his sphere of activity can be attended with profit. The time given to the new acquisition is so much waste, and his mental incapacity and absence of any moral interest in his work almost necessarily limits him to a single task. Thus, as we have seen, the many attempts to develop varied forms of production in the Southern colonies all failed. Maryland and Virginia grew only tobacco. South Carolina grew mainly rice. Moreover, the spectacle of the free laborer working on the same soil and at the same task, would be fatal to that resignation, and that complete moral and intellectual subjection, which alone can make slave labor possible. Thus the cheaper and more efficient system obtained the mastery so completely that by the beginning of the eighteenth century slave and negro had become well-nigh synonymous terms.

NEW ENGLAND BEFORE THE PILGRIM FATHERS LANDED

(1614)

BY CAPTAIN JOHN SMITH[1]

In the moneth of Aprill, 1614, with two Ships from London, of a few Marchants, I chanced to arriue in New-England, a parte of Ameryca, at the Ile of Monahiggan, in 43½ of northerly latitude: our plot was there to take Whales and make tryalls of a Myne of Gold and Copper. If those failed, Fish and Furres was then our refuge, to make our selues sauers howsoeuer: we found this Whale-fishing a costly conclusion: we saw many, and spent much time in chasing them; but could not kill any: They beeing a kinde of Iubartes, and not the Whale that yeeldes Finnes and Oyle as wee expected. For our Golde, it was rather the Masters deuice to get a voyage that proiected it, then any knowledge hee had at all of any such matter. Fish & Furres was now our guard: & by our late arriual, and long lingring about the Whale, the prime of both those seasons were past ere wee perceiued it; we thinking that their seasons serued

---

[1] From Smith's "Description of New England," published in London in 1616. Smith's exploration of New England was made after he had become separated from the Jamestown colony, of which in 1608, he had been president. He went there under an engagement with London merchants to fish for cod, barter for furs and explore the country for settlement. It was he who at the request of Prince Charles named the country New England.

at all times: but wee found it otherwise; for, by the midst of Iune, the fishing failed.

Yet in Iuly and August some was taken, but not sufficient to defray so great a charge as our stay required. Of dry fish we made about 40000. of Cor fish about 7000.

Whilest the sailers fished, my selfe with eight or nine others of them might best bee spared; Ranging the coast in a small boat. wee got for trifles neer 1100 Beuer skinnes, 100 Martins, and neer as many Otters; and the most of them within the distance of twenty leagues. We ranged the Coast both East and West much furder; but Eastwards our commodities were not esteemed, they were so neare the French who affords them better: and right against vs in the Main was a Ship of Sir Frances Popphames, that had there such acquaintance, hauing many years vsed onely that porte, that the most parte there was had by him. And 40 leagues westwards were two French Ships, that had made there a great voyage by trade, during the time wee tryed those conclusions, not knowing the Coast, nor Saluages habitation. With these Furres, the Traine, and Corfish I returned for England in the Bark: where within six monthes after our departure from the Downes, we safe arriued back. The best of this fish was solde for fiue pound the hundreth, the rest by ill vsage betwixt three pound and fifty shillings. The other Ship staied to fit herselfe for Spaine with the dry fish which was sould, by the Sailers reporte that returned, at forty ryalls the quintall, each hundred weighing two quintalls and a halfe.

New England is that part of America in the Ocean Sea opposite to Noua Albyon in the South

Sea; discouered by the most memorable Sir Francis Drake in his voyage about the worlde. In regarde whereto this is stiled New England, beeing in the same latitude. New France, off it, is Northward: Southwardes is Virginia, and all the adioyning Continent, with New Grenada, New Spain, New Andolosia and the West Indies. Now because I haue beene so oft asked such strange questions, of the goodnesse and greatnesse of those spatious Tracts of land, how they can bee thus long vnknown, or not possessed by the Spaniard, and many such like demands; I intreat your pardons, if I chance to be too plaine, or tedious in relating my knowledge for plaine mens satisfaction.

That part wee call New England is betwixt the degrees of 41. and 45: but that parte this discourse speaketh of, stretcheth but from Penobscot to Cape Cod, some 75 leagues by a right line distant each from other: within which bounds I haue seene at least 40. seuerall habitations vpon the Sea Coast, and sounded about 25 excellent good Harbours; In many whereof there is ancorage for 500 sayle of ships of any burthen; in some of them for 5000: And more than 200 Iles ouergrowne with good timber, of diuers sorts of wood, which doe make so many harbours as requireth a longer time then I had, to be well discouered. . . .

And surely by reason of those sandy cliffes and cliffes of rocks, both which we saw so planted with Gardens and Corne fields, and so well inhabited with a goodly, strong and well proportioned people, besides the greatnesse of the Timber growing on them, the greatnesse of the fish and the moderate temper of the ayre (for of twentie fiue, not any was sicke, but two that were many yeares dis-

eased before they went, notwithstanding our bad
lodging and accidentall diet) who can but approue
this a most excellent place, both for health & fertility? And of all the foure parts of the world
that I haue yet seene not inhabited, could I haue
but meanes to transport a Colonie, I would rather
liue here than any where: and if it did not main-
taine it selfe, were wee but once indifferently well
fitted, let vs starue.

The maine Staple, from hence to bee extracted
for the present to produce the rest, is fish; which
howeuer it may seeme a mean and a base com-
moditie: yet who will but truely take the pains
and consider the sequell, I thinke will allow it well
worth the labour. . . .

First, the ground is so fertill, that questionlesse
it is capable of producing any Grain, Fruits, or
Seeds you will sow or plant, growing in the Regions afore named: But it may be, not euery kinde
to that perfection of delicacy; or some tender
plants may miscarie, because the Summer is not
so hot, and the winter is more colde in those parts
wee haue yet tryed neere the Sea side, then we
finde in the same height in Europe or Asia; Yet
I made a Garden vpon the top of a Rockie Ile in
43.½, 4 leagues from the Main, in May, that grew
so well, as it serued vs for sallets in Iune and Iuly.
All sorts of cattell may here be bred and fed in
the Iles, or Peninsulaes, securely for nothing. In
the Interim till they encrease if need be (obseru-
ing the seasons) I durst vndertake to haue corne
enough from the Saluages for 300 men, for a few
trifles; and if they should bee vntoward (as it is
most certaine they are) thirty or forty good men
will be sufficient to bring them all in subiection,

and make this prouision; if they vnderstand what they doe: 200 whereof may nine monethes in the yeare be imployed in making marchandable fish, till the rest prouide other necessaries, fit to furnish vs with other commodities. . . .

But, to returne a little more to the particulars of this Countrey, which I intermingle thus with my proiects and reasons, not being so sufficiently yet acquainted in those parts, to write fully the estate of the Sea, the Ayre, the Land, the Fruites, the Rocks, the People, the Gouernment, Religion, Territories, and Limitations, Friends, and Foes: but, as I gathered from the niggardly relations in a broken language to my vnderstanding, during the time I ranged those Countries &c. The most Northern part I was at, was the Bay of Penobscot, which is East and West, North and South, more than ten leagues; but such were my occasions, I was constrained to be satisfied of them I found in the Bay, that the Riuer ranne farre vp into the Land, and was well inhabited with many people, but they were from their habitations, either fishing among the Iles, or hunting the Lakes and Woods, for Deer and Beuers. The Bay is full of great Ilands, of one, two, six, eight, or ten miles in length, which diuides it into many faire and excellent good harbours. On the East of it, are the Tarrantines, their mortall enemies, where inhabit the French, as they report that liue with those people, as one nation or family. And Northwest of Pennobscot is Mecaddacut, at the foot of a high mountaine, a kinde of fortresse against the Tarrantines adioyning to the high mountaines of Pennobscot, against whose feet doth beat the Sea.

But ouer all the Land, Iles, or other impediments, you may well see them sixteene or eighteene leagues from their situation. Segocket is the next; then Nufconcus, Pemmaquid, and Sagadahock. Vp this Riuer where was the Westerne plantation are Aumuckcawgen, Kinnebeck, and diuers others, where there is planted some corne fields. Along this Riuer 40 or 50 miles, I saw nothing but great high cliffes of barren Rocks, ouergrowne with wood: but where the Saluages dwelt there the ground is exceeding fat & fertill. Westward of this Riuer, is the Countrey of Aucocisco, in the bottome of a large deepe Bay, full of many great Iles, which diuides it into many good harbours. Sowocotuck is the next, in the edge of a large sandy Bay, which hath many Rocks and Iles, but few good harbours, but for Barks, I yet know. But all this Coast to Pennobscot, and as farre I could see Eastward of it is nothing but such high craggy Cliffy Rocks & stony Iles that I wondered such great trees could growe vpon so hard foundations. It is a Countrie rather to affright, then delight one. And how to describe a more plaine spectacle of desolation or more barren I knowe not. Yet the Sea there is the strangest fish-pond I euer saw; and those barren Iles so furnished with good woods, springs, fruits, fish, and foule, that it makes mee thinke though the Coast be rockie, and thus affrightable; the Vallies, Plaines, and interior parts, may well (notwithstanding) be verie fertile.

But there is no kingdome so fertile hath not some part barren: and New England is great enough, to make many Kingdomes and Countries, were it all inhabited. As you passe the Coast still Westward, Accominticus and Passataquack are two conuenient harbors for small barks; and a good Countrie, within their craggie cliffs. Angoam is the next; This place might content a right curious iudgement: but there are many sands at the entrance of the harbor: and the worst is, it is inbayed too farre from the deepe Sea. Heere are many rising hilles, and on their tops and descents many corne fields, and delightfull groues. On the East, is an Ile of two or three leagues in length; the one halfe, plaine morish grasse fit for pasture, with many faire high groues of mulberrie trees gardens: and there is also Okes, Pines, and other woods to make this place an excellent habitation, beeing a good and safe harbor.

Naimkeck though it be more rockie ground (for Angoam is sandie) not much inferior; neither for the harbor, nor any thing I could perceiue, but the multitude of people. From hence doth stretch into the sea the faire headland Tragabigzanda, fronted with three Iles called the three Turks heads: to the North of this, doth enter a great Bay, where wee founde some habitations and corne fields: they report a great Riuer[2], and at least thirtie habitations, doo possesse this Countrie. But because the French had got their Trade, I had no leasure to discouer it.

The Iles of Mattahunts are on the West side of this Bay, where are many Iles, and questionlesse good harbors: and then the Countrie of the Massachusets, which is the Paradise of all those parts: for, heere are many Iles all planted with corne; groues, mulberries, saluage gardens, and good harbors: the Coast is for the most part, high clayie sandie cliffs. The Sea Coast as you passe, shewes

[2] Probably the Merrimac.

you all along large corne fields, and great troupes
of well proportioned people: but the French
hauing remained heere neere sixe weekes, left
nothing, for vs to take occasion to examine the inhabitants relations, viz, if there be neer three
thousand people vpon these Iles; and that the
Riuer doth pearce many daies iourneies the in-
tralles of that Countrey. We found the people in
those parts verie kinde; but in their furie no lesse
valiant. For, vpon a quarrell wee had with one
of them, hee onely with three others crossed the
harbor of Quonahassit to certaine rocks whereby
wee must passe; and there let flie their arrowes
for our shot, till we were out of danger.

Then come you to Accomack, an excellent good
harbor, good land; and no want of any thing, but
industrious people. After much kindnesse, vpon
a small occasion, wee fought also with fortie or
fiftie of those: though some were hurt, and some
slaine; yet within an houre after they became
friendes. Cape Cod is the next presents it selfe;
which is onely a headland of high hils of sand,
ouergrowne with shrubbie pines, hurts, and such
trash; but an excellent harbor for all weathers.
This Cape is made by the maine Sea on the one
side, and a great Bay on the other in forme of a
sickle: on it doth inhabit the people of Pawmet:
and in the bottome of the Bay, the people of
Chawum.

THE FIRST VOYAGE OF THE "MAYFLOWER"

(1620)

BY GOVERNOR WILLIAM BRADFORD [1]

Sept^r: 6. These troubls being blowne over, and now all being compacte togeather in one shipe, they put to sea againe with a prosperus winde, which continued diverce days togeather, which was some incouragemente unto them; yet according to ye usuall maner many were afflicted with sea-sicknes. . . .

After they had injoyed faire winds and weather for a season, they were incountred many times with crosse winds, and mette with many feirce stormes, with which ye ship was shroudly shaken,

[1] William Bradford had already been a leading member of a little dissenting congregation in England, when, in 1608, it fled from England to Holland, and in 1620 settled at Plymouth, Mass. A year after the arrival at Plymouth Bradford was elected Governor of the Colony, and, with the exception of two short intervals, held this office until his death nearly forty years afterward.

Bradford's "History of Plymouth" is a classic in New England historical literature—the foundation-stone, in fact, of the history of New England. A curious item in the survival of the manuscript is that, at the time of the evacuation of Boston by the British, during the Revolution, it disappeared mysteriously, to be discovered eighty years afterward in the palace of the Bishop of London. More than forty years after this discovery, the manuscript was restored by the diocese of London to the commonwealth of Massachusetts, which now preserves it in the State Library in Boston.

and her upper works made very leakie; and one of the maine beames in ye midd ships was bowed & craked, which put them in some fear that ye shipe could not be able to performe ye vioage. So some of ye cheefe of ye company, perceiving ye mariners to feare ye suffisiencie of ye shipe, as appeared by their mutterings, they entred into serious consulltation with ye m^r. & other officers of ye ship, to consider in time of ye danger; and rather to returne then to cast them selves into a desperate & inevitable perill. And truly ther was great distraction & differance of opinion amongst ye mariners themselves; faine would they doe what could be done for their wages sake, (being now halfe the seas over,) and on ye other hand they were loath to hazard their lives too desperatly. But in examening of all opinions, the m^r. & others affirmed they knew ye ship to be stronge & firme under water; and for the buckling of ye maine beame, ther was a great iron scrue ye passengers brought out of Holland, which would raise ye beame into his place; ye which being done, the carpenter & m^r. affirmed that with a post put under it, set firme in ye lower deck, & otherways bounde, he would make it sufficiente.

And as for ye decks & uper workes they would calke them as well as they could, and though with ye workeing of ye ship they would not longe keepe stanch, yet ther would otherwise be no great danger, if they did not overpress her with sails. So they comited them selves to ye will of God, & resolved to proseede. In sundrie of these stormes the winds were so feirce, & ye seas so high, as they could not beare a knote of saile, but were forced to hull, for diverce days togither. And in one of them, as they thus lay at hull, in a mighty storme, a lustie yonge man (called John Howland) coming upon some occasion above ye grattings, was, with a seele of ye shipe throwne into [y^e] sea; but it pleased God y^t he caught hould of ye tope-saile halliards, which hunge over board, & rane out at length; yet he held his hould (though he was sundrie fadomes under water) till he was hald up by ye same rope to ye brime of ye water, and then with a boat hooke & other means got into ye shipe againe, & his life saved; and though he was something ill with it, yet he lived many years after, and became a profitable member both in church & comone wealthe. In all this siage ther died but one of ye passengers, which was William Butten, a youth, servant to Samuel Fuller, when they drew near ye coast. . . .

But to omite other things, (that I may be breefe,) after longe beating at sea they fell with that land which is called Cape Cod; the which being made & certainly knowne to be it, they were not a little joyfull. After some deliberation had amongst them selves & with ye m^r. of ye ship, they tacked aboute and resolved to stande for ye southward (ye wind & weather being faire) to find some place aboute Hudsons river for their habitation. But after they had sailed y^t course aboute half ye day, they fell amongst deangerous shoulds and roring breakers, and they were so farr intangled ther with as they conceived them selves in great danger; & ye wind shrinking upon them withall, they resolved to bear up againe for the Cape, and thought them selves hapy to gett out of those dangers before night overtooke them, as by Gods providence they did. And y⁰ next day they gott into y⁰ Cape-harbor wher they ridd in saftie.² A word or too by y⁰ way of this cape; it was thus first named by Capten Gosnole & his company, An⁰: 1602, and after by Capten Smith was caled Cape James; but it retains y⁰ former name amongst sea-men. Also y¹ pointe which first shewed those dangerous shoulds unto them, they called Point Care, & Tuckers Terrour; but y¹ French & Dutch to this day call it Malabarr, by reason of those perilous shoulds, and y⁰ losses they have suffered their.

Being thus arived in a good harbor and brought safe to land, they fell upon their knees & blessed y⁰ God of heaven, who had brought them over y⁰ vast & furious ocean, and delivered them from all y⁰ periles & miseries thereof, againe to set their feete on y⁰ firme and stable earth, their proper elemente. And no marvell if they were thus joyefull, seeing wise Seneca was so affected with sailing a few miles on y⁰ coast of his owne Italy; as he affirmed, that he had rather remaine twentie years on his way by land, then pass by sea to any place in a short time; so tedious & dreadfull was y⁰ same unto him. . . .

But hear I cannot but stay and make a pause, and stand half amased at this poore peoples presente condition; and so I thinke will the reader too, when he well considers y⁰ same. Being

² Now known as Provincetown, where a lofty monument on a hill back of the harbor, dedicated in 1910, commemorates the landing there of the Pilgrim Fathers. While the Mayflower lay in this harbor, Paregrine White was born, the first child of English parentage born in New England.

thus passed ye vast ocean, and a sea of troubles before in their preparation (as may be remembred by y^t which wente before), they had now no freinds to well come them, nor inns to entertaine or refresh their weatherbeaten bodys, no houses or much less townes to repaire too, to seeke for succoure. It is recorded in scripture as a mercie to ye apostle & his shipwraked company, y^t the barbarians shewed them no smale kindnes in refreshing them, but these savage barbarians, when they mette with them (as after will appeare) were readier to fill their sids full of arrows then otherwise. And for ye season it was winter, and they that know ye winters of y^t cuntrie know them to be sharp & violent, & subjecte to cruell & feirce stormes, deangerous to travill to known places, much more to serch an unknown coast. Besids, what could they see but a hidious & desolate wilderness, full of wild beasts & willd men? and what multituds ther might be of them they knew not. Nether could they, as it were, goe up to ye tope of Pisgah, to vew from this willdernes a more goodly cuntrie to feed their hops; for which way soever they turnd their eys (save upward to ye heavens) they could have little solace or content in respecte of any outward objects.

For sumer being done, all things stand upon them with a wetherbeaten face; and ye whole countrie, full of woods & thickets, represented a wild & savage view. If they looked behind them, ther was ye mighty ocean which they had passed, and was now as a maine barr & goulfe to seperate them from all ye civil parts of ye world. If it be said they had a ship to sucour them, it is trew; but what heard they daly from ye m^r. & company? but y^t with speede they should looke out a place with their shallop, wher they would be at some near distance; for ye season was shuch as he would not stirr from thence till a safe harbor was discovered by them wher they would be, and he might goe without danger; and that victells consumed apace, but he must & would keepe sufficient for them selves & their returne. Yea, it was muttered by some, that if they gott not a place in time, they would turne them & their goods ashore & leave them.

Let it also be considred what weake hopes of supply & succoure they left behinde them, y^t might bear up their minds in this sade condition and trialls they were under; and they could not but be very smale. It is true, indeed, ye affections & love of their brethren at Leyden was cordiall & entire towards them, but they had litle power to help them, or them selves; and how ye case stode between them & ye marchants at their coming away, hath allready been declared. What could now sustaine them but ye spirite of God & his grace? . . .

Being thus arrived at Cape-Codd ye 11. of November, and necessitie calling them to looke out a place for habitation, (as well as the maisters & mariners importunitie,) they having brought a large shalop with them out of England, stowed in quarters in ye ship, they now gott her out & sett their carpenters to worke to trime her up; but being much brused & shatered in ye shipe wth foule weather, they saw she would be longe in mending. Whereupon a few of them tendered them selves to goe by land and discovere those nearest places, whilst ye shallop was in mending; and ye rather because as they wente into y^t harbor ther seemed to be an opening some 2. or 3. leagues of, which ye maister judged to be a river. It was conceived ther might be some danger in ye attempte yet seeing them resolute, they were permited to goe, being 16. of them well armed, under ye conduct of Captain Standish, having shuch instructions given them as was thought meete.

They sett forth ye 15. of Nove^{br}: and when they had marched aboute ye space of a mile by ye sea side, they espied 5. or 6. persons with a dogg coming towards them, who were salvages; but they fled from them, & rane up into ye woods, and ye English followed them, partly to see if they could speake with them, and partly to discover if ther might not be more of them lying in ambush. But ye Indeans seeing them selyes thus followed, they again forsooke the woods, & rane away on ye sands as hard as they could, so as they could not come near them, but followed them by ye tracte of their feet sundrie miles, and saw that they had come the same way. So, night coming on, they made their randevous & set out ther sentinels, and rested in quiete ye night, and the next morning followed their tracte till they had headed a great creeke, & so left the sands, & turned an other way into ye woods. But they still followed them by geuss, hopeing to find their dwellings; but they soone lost both them & them selves, falling into shuch thickets as were ready to tear their cloaths & armore in peeces, but were most distressed for wante of drinke.

But at length they found water & refreshed

them selves, being ye first New-England water
they drunke of, and was now in thir great thirste
as pleasante unto them as wine or bear had been
in for-times. Afterwards they directed their
course to come to ye other shore, for they knew
it was a necke of land they were to crosse over,
and so at length gott to ye sea-side, and marched
to this supposed river, & by ye way found a pond
of clear fresh water, and shortly after a good
quantitie of clear ground wher ye Indeans had
formerly set corne, and some of their graves. And
proceeding furder they saw new-stuble wher corne
had been set ye same year, also they found wher
latly a house had been, wher some planks and a
great ketle was remaining, and heaps of sand
newly padled with their hands, which they, dig-
ging up, found in them diverce faire Indean
baskets filled with corne, and some in eares, faire
and good, of diverce collours, which seemed to
them a very goodly sight, (haveing never seen any
shuch before).

The month of November being spente in these
affairs, & much foule weather falling in, the 6.
of Desem^r: they sente out their shallop againe
with 10. of their principall men, & some sea
men, upon further discovery, intending to circu-
later that deepe bay of Cape-Codd. The weather
was very could, & it frose so hard as ye sprea of
ye sea lighting on their coats, they were as if
they had been glased; yet that night betimes they
gott downe into ye botome of ye bay, and as they
drue nere ye shore they saw some 10. or 12. Indeans very busie aboute some thing. They landed
about a league or 2. from them, and had much
a doe to put a shore any wher, it lay so full of

flats. Being landed, it grew late, and they made themselves a barricade with loggs & bowes as well as they could in ye time, & set out their sentenill & betooke them to rest, and saw ye smoake of ye fire ye savages made y^t night.

When morning was come they devided their company, some to coast alonge ye shore in ye boate, and the rest marched throw ye woods to see ye land, if any fit place might be for their dwelling. They came also to ye place wher they saw the Indeans ye night before, & found they had been cuting up a great fish like a grampus, being some 2. inches thike of fate like a hogg, some peeces wher of they had left by ye way; and ye shallop found 2. more of these fishes dead on ye sands, thing usuall after storms in y^t place, by reason of ye great flats of sand that lye of. So they ranged up and doune all y^t day, but found no people, nor any place they liked. When ye sune grue low, they hasted out of ye woods to meete with their shallop, to whom them made signes to come to them into a creeke hardby, which they did at high-water; of which they were very glad, for they had not seen each other all y^t day, since ye morning.

So they made them a barricado (as usually they did every night) with loggs, staks, & thike pine bowes, ye height of a man, leaving it open to lee-ward, partly to shelter them from ye could & wind (making their fire in ye midle, & lying round aboute it), and partly to defend them from any sudden assaults of ye savags, if they should surround them. So being very weary, they betooke them to rest. But about midnight they heard a hideous & great crie, and their sentinall caled,

"Arme, arme"; so they bestired them & stood to their armes, & shote of a cupple of moskets, and then the noys seased. They concluded it was a companie of wolves, or such like willd beasts; for one of ye sea men tould them he had often heard shuch a noyse in New-found land. So they rested till about 5. of ye clock in the morning; for ye tide, & ther purposs to goe from thence, made them be stiring betimes. So after praier they prepared for breakfast, and it being day dawning, it was thought best to be carring things downe to ye boate. But some said it was not best to carrie ye armes downe, others said they would be the readier, for they had laped them up in their coats from ye dew.

But some 3. or 4. would not cary theirs till they wente them selves, yet as it fell out, ye water being not high enough, they layed them downe on ye banke side, & came up to breakfast. But presently, all on ye sudain, they heard a great & strange crie, which they knew to be the same voyces they heard in ye night, though they varied their notes, and & one of their company being abroad came runing in, & cried, "Men, Indeans, Indeans"; and wth all, their arowes came flying amongst them. Their men rane with all speed to recover their armes, as by ye good providence of God they did. In ye mean time, of those that were ther ready, two muskets were discharged at them, & 2. more stood ready in ye entrance of ther randevoue, but were comanded not to shoote till they could take full aime at them; & ye other 2. charged againe with all speed, for ther were only 4. had armes ther, & defended ye baricado which was first assalted. The crie of y^e

Indeans was dreadfull, espetially when they saw ther men rune out of yᵉ randevoue towourds yᵉ shallop, to recover their armes, the Indeans wheeling aboute upon them. But some runing out with coats of malle on, & cutlasses in their hands, they soone got their armes, & let flye amongs them, and quickly stopped their violence.

Yet ther was a lustie man, and no less valiante, stood behind a tree within halfe a musket shot, and let his arrows flie at them. He was seen shoot 3. arrowes, which were all avoyded. He stood 3. shot of a musket, till one taking full aime at him, and made yᵉ barke or splinters of yᵉ tree fly about his ears, after which he gave an extraordinary shrike, and away they wente all of them. They left some to keep yᵉ shalope, and followed them aboute a quarter of a mile, and shouted once or twise, and shot of 2. or 3. peces, & so returned. This they did, that they might conceive that they were not affrade of them or any way discouraged. Thus it pleased God to vanquish their enimies, and give them deliverance; and by his spetiall providence so to dispose that not any one of them were either hurte, or hitt, though their arrows came close by them, & on every side them, and sundry of their coats which hunge up in yᵉ barricado, were shot throw & throw. Aterwards they gave God sollamme thanks & praise for their deliverance, & gathered up a bundle of their arrows, & sente them into England afterward by yᵉ mʳ. of yᵉ ship, and called that place yᵉ first encounter.

From hence they departed, and costed all along, but discerned no place likly for harbor; & therfore hasted to a place that their pillote, (one

M^r. Coppin who had bine in ye cuntrie before)
did assure them was a good harbor, which he had
been in, and they might fetch it before night;
of which they were glad, for it begane to be foule
weather. After some houres sailing, it begane to
snow & raine, & about ye midle of ye afternoone,
ye wind increased, & ye sea became very rough,
and they broake their rudder, & it was as much
as 2. men could doe to steere her with a cupple
of oares. But their pillott bad them be of good
cheere, for he saw ye harbor; but ye storme increasing, & night drawing on, they bore what
saile they could to gett in, while they could see.
But herwith they broake their mast in 3 peeces,
& their saill fell over bord, in a very grown sea,
so as they had like to have been cast away; yet
by Gods mercie they recovered themselves, &
having ye floud with them, struck into ye harbore.
But when it came too, ye pillott was deceived in
ye place, and said, ye Lord be merciful unto them,
for his eys never saw y^t place before; & he & the
m^r. mate would have rune her ashore, in a cove
full of breakers, before ye winde. But a lusty
seaman which steered, bad those which rowed, if
they were men, about with her, or ells they
were all cast away; the which they did with
speed. So he bid them be of good cheere & row
lustly, for ther was a faire sound before them,
& he doubted not but they should find one place
or other wher they might ride in saftie.

And though it was very darke, and rained sore,
yet in ye end they gott under ye lee of a smalle
iland, and remained ther all y^t night saftie. But
they knew not this to be an iland till morning,
but were devided into their minds; some would

keepe yᵉ boate for fear they might be amongst yᵉ Indians; others were so weake and could, they could not endure, but got ashore, & with much adoe got fire, (all things being so wett,) and yᵉ rest were glad to come to them; for after midnight yᵉ wind shifted to the north-west, & it frose hard. But though this had been a day & night of much trouble & danger unto them, yet God gave them a morning of comforte and refreshing (as usually he doth to his children), for yᵉ next day was a faire sunshinig day, and they found them selvs to be on an iland secure from yᵉ Indeans, wher they might drie their stufe, fixe their peeces, & rest them selves, and gave God thanks for his mercies, in their manifould deliverances. And this being the last day of yᵉ weeke, they prepared ther to keepe yᵉ Sabath. On Munday they sounded yᵉ harbor, and founde it fitt for shipping; and marched into yᵉ land, & found diverse cornfeilds, & little runing brooks, a placed (as they supposed) fitt for situation; at least it was yᵉ best they could find, and yᵉ season, & their presente necessitie, made them glad to accept of it. So they returned to their shipp againe with this news to yᵉ rest of their people, which did much comforte their harts.

On yᵉ 15. of Desemʳ. they wayed anchor to goe to yᵉ place they had discovered, & came within 2. leagues of it, but were faine to bear up againe; but ye 16. day yᵉ winde came faire, and they arrived safe in this harbor.[3] And afterwards took better view of yᵉ place, and resolved wher to pitch their dwelling; and yᵉ 25. day begane to

---

[3] The landing at Plymouth was effected on December 21.

erecte yᵉ first house for comone use to receive them and their goods. . . .

I shall a litle returne backe and begine with a combination made by them before they came ashore, being yᵉ first foundation of their governmente in this place; occasioned partly by yᵉ discontented and mutinous speeches that some of the strangers amongst them had let fall from them in yᵉ ship—That when they came ashore they would use their own libertie; for none had power to comand them, the patente they had being for Virginia, and not for New-england, which belonged to an other Government, with which yᵉ Virginia Company had nothing to doe. And partly that shuch an acte by them done (this their condition considered) might be as firme as any patent, and in some respects more sure. The forme was as followeth:

"In yᵉ name of God, Amen. We whose names are underwriten, the loyall subjects of our dread soveraigne Lord, King James, by yᵉ Grace of God, of Great Britaine, Franc, & Ireland king, defender of yᵉ faith, &c., having undertaken, for yᵉ glorie of God, and advancemente of yᵉ Christian faith, and honour of our king & countrie, a voyage to plant yᵉ first colonie in ye Northerne parts of Virginia, doe by these presents solemnly & mutualy in yᵉ presence of God, and one of another, covenant & combine our selves together into a civill body politick, for our better ordering & preservation & furtherance of yᵉ ends aforesaid; and by vertue hearof to enacte, constitute, and frame such just & equall lawes, ordinances, acts, constitutions, & offices, from time to time, as shall be thought most meete & convenient for yᵉ gen-

erall good of yᵉ Colonie, unto which we promise
all due submission and obedience. In witness
wherof we have hereunder subscribed our names
at Cape-Codd yᵉ 11. of November, in yᵉ year of
England, Franc, & Ireland ye eighteenth, and of
Scotland yᵉ fiftie fourth.   Anᵒ: Dom. 1620.''

THE FIRST NEW YORK SETTLE-
MENTS

(1623-1628)

BY NICHOLAS JEAN DE WASSENAER[1]

We treated in our preceding discourse of the discovery of some rivers in Virginia; the studious reader will learn how affairs proceeded. The West India Company being chartered to navigate these rivers, did not neglect so to do, but equipped in the spring [of 1623] a vessel of 130 lasts, called the *New Netherland* whereof Cornelis Jacobs of Hoorn was skipper, with 30 families, mostly Walloons, to plant a colony there. They sailed in the beginning of March, and directing their course by the Canary Islands, steered towards

[1] From Wassenaer's "Description of the first settlement of New Netherland." Printed in Hart's "American History Told by Contemporaries." Wassenaer was a Dutchman, and wrote contemporaneously with the events he describes. After Hudson's discovery of the Hudson River, Dutch ships were sent over to Manhattan Island to establish an agency for the collection of furs. Rude cabins were pitched and lived in at the southern end of the island, but these did not constitute a permanent settlement; they were a mere trading-post. The trade became so profitable, however, that something more permanent was desired, and in 1623 the West India Company dispatched ships with thirty families as the nucleus of a colony to be established near the present site of Albany. Not until two years later was it decided that the headquarters of the colony should be on Manhattan Island. Two ships were then sent out to establish there a permanent and more extensive settlement.

the wild coast, and gained the westwind which luckily (took) them in the beginning of May into the river called, first Rio de Montagnes, now the river Mauritius, lying in 40½ degrees. He found a Frenchman lying in the mouth of the river, who would erect the arms of the King of France there; but the Hollanders would not permit him, opposing it by commission from the Lords States General and the directors of the West India Company; and in order not to be frustrated therein, with the assistance of those of the *Mackerel* which lay above, they caused a yacht of 2 guns to be manned, and convoyed the Frenchman out of the river, who would do the same thing in the south river, but he was also prevented by the settlers there. This being done, the ship sailed up to the Maykans, 44 miles, near which they built and completed a fort named "Orange," with 4 bastions, on an island, by them called Castle Island. . . .

Respecting these colonies, they have already a prosperous beginning; and the hope is that they will not fall through provided they be zealously sustained, not only in that place but in the South river. For their increase and prosperous advancement, it is highly necessary that those sent out be first of all well provided with means both of support and defense, and that being freemen, they be settled there on a free tenure; that all they work for and gain be theirs to dispose of and to sell it according to their pleasure; that whoever is placed over them as commander act as their father not as their executioner, leading them with a gentle hand; for whoever rules them as a friend and associate will be beloved by them, as he who will order them as a superior will subvert and nullify everything;

yea, they will excite against him the neighbouring provinces to which they will fly. 'Tis better to rule by love and friendship than by force. . . .

As the country is well adapted for agriculture and the raising of every thing that is produced here, the aforesaid Lords resolved to take advantage of the circumstances, and to provide the place with many necessaries, through the Honble. Pieter Evertsen Hulst, who undertook to ship thither, at his risk, whatever was requisite, to wit: one hundred and three head of cattle; stallions, mares, steers and cows, for breeding and multiplying, besides all the hogs and sheep that might be thought expedient to send thither; and to distribute these in two ships of one hundred and forty lasts, in such a manner that they should be well foddered and attended to. . . .

In company with these, goes a fast sailing vessel at the risk of the directors. In these aforesaid vessels also go six complete families with some freemen, so that forty five newcomers or inhabitants are taken out, to remain there. The natives of New Netherland are very well disposed so long as no injury is done them. But if any wrong be committed against them they think it long till they be revenged. . . .

They are a wicked, bad people, very fierce in arms. Their dogs are small. When the Honble. Lambrecht van Twenhuyzen, once a skipper, had given them a big dog, and it was presented to them on ship-board, they were very much afraid of it; calling it, also a Sachem of dogs, being the biggest. The dog, tied with a rope on board, was very furious against them, they being clad like beasts with skins, for he thought they were game; but when they gave him some of their bread made of Indian corn, which grows there, he learned to distinguish them, that they were men.

The Colony was planted at this time, on the Manhates where a Fort was staked out by Master Kryn Frederycke, an engineer. It will be of large dimensions. . . .

The government over the people of New Netherland continued on the 19th of August of this year in the aforesaid Minuit, successor to Verhulst, who went thither from Holand on 9th January, Anno, 1626, and took up his residence in the midst of a nation called Manhates, building a fort there, to be called Amsterdam, having four points and faced outside entirely with stone, as the walls of sand fall down, and are now more compact.

The population consists of two hundred and seventy souls, including men, women, and children. They remained as yet without the Fort, in no fear, as the natives live peaceably with them. They are situate three miles from the Sea, on the river by us called Mauritius, by others, Rio de Montagne. . . .

After the Right Honble Lords Directors of the Privileged West India Company in the United Netherlands, had provided for the defence of New Netherland and put everything there in good order, they taking into consideration the advantages of said place, the favorable nature of the air, and soil, and that considerable trade and goods and many commodities may be obtained from thence, sent some persons, of their own accord, thither with all sorts of cattle and implements necessary for agriculture, so that in the year 1628 there already resided on the island of the Manhates, two hundred and seventy souls, men, women, and children, under Governor Minuit, Verhulst's successor, living there in peace with the natives. But as the land, in many places being full of weeds and wild productions, could not be properly cultivated in consequence of the scantiness of the population, the said Lords Directors of the West India Company, the better to people their lands, & to bring the country to produce more abundantly, resolved to grant divers privileges, freedoms, and exemptions to all patroons, masters or individuals who should plant any colonies and cattle in New Netherland, and they accordingly have constituted and published in print (certain) exemptions, to afford better encouragement and infuse greater zeal into whomsoever should be inclined to reside and plant his colonie in New Netherland.

THE SWEDES AND DUTCH IN NEW JERSEY AND DELAWARE

(1627)

BY ISRAEL ACRELIUS[1]

After that the magnanimous Genoese Christopher Columbus, had, at the expense of Ferdinand, King of Spain, in the year 1492, discovered the Western hemisphere, and the illustrious Florentine, Americus Vespucius, sent out by King Emanuel of Portugal, in the year 1502, to make a further exploration of its coasts, had had the good fortune to give the country his name, the European powers have, from time to time, sought to promote their several interests there. Our Swedes and Goths were the less backward in such expeditions, as they had always been the first therein. They had already, in the year 996 after the birth of Christ, visited America, had named it Vinland the Good, and also Skrællinga Land, and had called its inhabitants "the Skrællings of Vinland." It is therefore evident that the Northmen had visited some part of North America be-

---

[1] From Acrelius's "History of New Sweden." Printed in "Old South Leaflets." Acrelius from 1749 until 1756 was provost over Swedish Congregations in America and pastor of their church at Christina, now Wilmington, on the Delaware. His complete work is an exhaustive one, and covers not only the early but the later years of Swedish history on the Delaware. It has long been esteemed the best work we have on the subject.

fore the Spaniards and Portuguese went to South
America. . . .

From that time until 1623, when the West India
Company obtained its charter, their trade with
the Indians was conducted almost entirely on ship-
board, and they made no attempts to build any
house or fortress until 1629. Now, whether that
was done with or without the permission of England, the town of New Amsterdam was built and
fortified, as also the place Aurania, Orange, now
called Albany, having since had three general-
governors, one after the other. But that was not
yet enough. They wished to extend their power
to the river Delaware also, and erected on its
shores two or three small forts, which were, however, soon after destroyed by the natives of the
country.

It now came in order for Sweden also to take
part in this enterprise. William Usselinx,[2] a Hollander, born at Antwerp in Brabant, presented
himself to King Gustaf Adolph, and laid before
him a proposition for a Trading Company, to be
established in Sweden, and to extend its operations to Asia, Africa, and Magellan's Land (Terra
Magellanica), with the assurance that this would
be a great source of revenue to the kingdom. Full
power was given him to carry out this important
project; and thereupon a contract of trade was
drawn up, to which the Company was to agree
and subscribe it. Usselinx published explanations
of this contract, wherein he also particularly directed attention to the country on the Delaware,

[2] Usselinx had proposed the formation of a company to
trade in foreign countries, including America, as early as
1604.

107

its fertility, convenience, and all its imaginable
resources. To strengthen the matter, a charter
(octroy) was secured for the Company, and especially to Usselinx, who was to receive a royalty of
one thousandth upon all articles bought or sold by
the Company.

The powerful king, whose zeal for the honor of
God was not less ardent than for the welfare of
his subjects, availed himself of this opportunity
to extend the doctrines of Christ among the heath-
en, as well as to establish his own power in other
parts of the world. To this end he sent forth
Letters Patent, dated at Stockholm on the 2d of
July, 1626, wherein all, both high and low, were
invited to contribute something to the Company,
according to their means. The work was completed in the Diet of the following year, 1627,
when the estates of the realm gave their assent,
and confirmed the measure. . . .

But when these arrangements were now in full
progress, and duly provided for, the German war
and the king's death occurred, which caused this
important work to be laid aside. The Trading
Company was dissolved, its subscriptions nullified,
and the whole project seemed about to die with
the king. But, just as it appeared to be at its
end, it received new life. Another Hollander by
the name of Peter Menewe, sometimes called Menuet,[3] made his appearance in Sweden.

As a good beginning, the first colony was sent
off; and Peter Menewe was placed over it, as
being best acquainted in those regions. They set

---

[3] Peter Minuit, the Governor of New Amsterdam, who purchased Manhattan Island from the Indians for goods worth
$24, is here referred to.

sail from Götheborg, in a ship-of-war called the *Key of Colmar,* followed by a smaller vessel bearing the name of the *Bird Griffin,* both laden with people, provisions, ammunition, and merchandise, suitable for traffic and gifts to the Indians. The ships successfully reached their place of destination. The high expectations which our emigrants had of that new land were well met by the first views which they had of it. They made their first landing on the bay or entrance to the river Poutaxat, which they called the river of New Sweden; and the place where they landed they called Paradise Point.[4]

A purchase of land was immediately made from the Indians; and it was determined that all the land on the western side of the river, from the point called Cape Inlopen or Hinlopen,[5] up to the fall called Santickan, and all the country inland, as much as was ceded, should belong to the Swedish crown forever. Posts were driven into the ground as landmarks, which were still seen in their places sixty years afterward. A deed was drawn up for the land thus purchased. This was written in Dutch, because no Swede was yet able to interpret the language of the heathen. The Indians subscribed their hands and marks. The writing was sent home to Sweden to be preserved

[4] Paradise Point was near the present town of Lewes, in the State of Delaware. The site is near where the Bay merges in the ocean.

[5] This name has been corrupted into Henlopen. The cape was named by Captain Cornelius Mey after a town in Friesland. Mey's name was given to the southern point of New Jersey now known as Cape May. He visited Delaware Bay in or about 1614.

in the royal archives. Mans Kling was the surveyor. He laid out the land and made a map of the whole river, with its tributaries, islands, and points, which is still to be found in the royal archives in Sweden. Their clergyman was Reorus Torkillus of East Gothland.

The first abode of the newly arrived emigrants was at a place called by the Indians Hopokahacking. There, in the year 1638, Peter Menuet built a fortress which he named Fort Christina, after the reigning queen of Sweden.[6] The place, situated upon the west side of the river, was probably chosen so as to be out of the way of the Hollanders, who claimed the eastern side,—a measure of prudence, until the arrival of a greater force from Sweden. The fort was built upon an eligible site, not far from the mouth of the creek, so as to secure them in the navigable water of the Maniquas, which was afterward called Christina Kihl, or creek.

Peter Menuet made a good beginning for the settlement of the Swedish colony in America. He guarded his little fort for over three years, and the Hollanders neither attempted nor were able to overthrow it. After some years of faithful service he died at Christina. In his place followed Peter Hollendare, a native Swede, who did not remain at the head of its affairs more than a year and a half. He returned home to Sweden, and was a major at Skkepsholm, in Stockholm, in the year 1655.

---

[6] Ft. Christina was within the limits of the present city of Wilmington. The ancient Swedish church, built in 1698 and still standing in Wilmington, marks the site of this, the original settlement of Swedes in Delaware.

The second emigration took place under Lieutenant Colonel John Printz, who went out with the appointment of Governor of New Sweden. He had a grant of four hundred rix dollars for his traveling expenses, and one thousand two hundred dollars silver as his annual salary. The Company was invested with the exclusive privilege of importing tobacco into Sweden, altho that article was even then regarded as unnecessary and injurious, altho indispensable since the establishment of the bad habit of its use. Upon the same occasion was also sent out Magister John Campanius Holm, who was called by their excellencies the Royal Council and Admiral Claes Flemming, to become the government chaplain, and watch over the Swedish congregation.

The ship on which they sailed was called the *Fama*. It went from Stockholm to Götheborg, and there took in its freight. Along with this went two other ships of the line, the *Swan* and the *Charitas*, laden with people, and other necessaries. Under Governor Printz, ships came to the colony in three distinct voyages. The first ship was the *Black Cat*, with ammunition, and merchandise for the Indians. Next, the ship *Swan*, on a second voyage, with emigrants, in the year 1647. Afterward, two other ships, called the *Key* and the *Lamp*. During these times the clergymen, Mr. Lawrence Charles Lockenius and Mr. Israel Holgh, were sent out to the colony. . . .

The voyage to New Sweden was at that time quite long. The watery way to the West was not yet well discovered, and, therefore, for fear of the sand-banks off Newfoundland, they kept their course to the east and south as far as to what were then called the Brazates. The ships which went under the command of Governor Printz sailed along the coast of Portugal, and down the coast of Africa, until they found the eastern passage, then directly over to America, leaving the Canaries high up to the north. They landed at Antigua, then continued their voyage northward, past Virginia and Maryland, to Cape Hinlopen. Yet, in view of the astonishingly long route which they took, the voyage was quick enough in six months' time,—from Stockholm on August 16, 1642, to the new fort of Christina, in New Sweden, on February 15, 1643.

The Swedes who emigrated to America belonged partly to a trading company, provided with a charter, who for their services, according to their condition of agreement, were to receive pay and monthly wages; a part of them also went on their own impulse to try their fortune. For these it was free to settle and live in the country as long as they pleased or to leave it, and they were therefore, by way of distinction from the others, called freemen. At first, also, malefactors and vicious people were sent over, who were used as slaves to labor upon the fortifications. They were kept in chains and not allowed to have intercourse with the other settlers; moreover, a separate place of abode was assigned to them. The neighboring people and country were dissatisfied that such wretches should come into the colony. It was also, in fact, very objectionable in regard to the heathen, who might be greatly offended by it. Whence it happened that, when such persons came over in Governor Printz's time, it was not permitted that one of them should set foot upon the shore, but they had all to be carried back again, whereupon a great part of them died during the voyage or perished in some other way. Afterward it was forbidden at home in Sweden, under a penalty, to take for the American voyage any persons of bad fame; nor was there ever any lack of good people for the colony.

Governor Printz was now in a position to put the government upon a safe footing to maintain the rights of the Swedes, and to put down the attempts of the Hollanders. They had lately, before his arrival, patched their little Fort Nassau. On this account he selected the island of Tenac-kong as his residence, which is sometimes also called Tutaeaenung and Tenicko, about three Swedish miles from Fort Christina. The convenient situation of the place suggested its selection as also the location of Fort Nassau,[7] which lay some miles over against it, to which he could thus command the passage by water. The new fort, which was erected and provided with considerable armament, was called New Götheborg. His place of residence, which he adorned with orchards, gardens, a pleasure-house, etc., he named Printz Hall. A handsome wooden church was also built at the same place, which Magister Campanius consecrated, on the last great prayer-day which was celebrated in New Sweden, on the 4th of September, 1646. Upon that place also all the most prominent freemen had their residences and plantations.

[7] Fort Nassau was on Delaware Bay at the mouth of Timber Creek, below Gloucester Point, in New Jersey.

THE BEGINNINGS OF THE MASSA-CHUSETTS BAY COLONY

(1627—1631)

BY GOVERNOR THOMAS DUDLEY[1]

Touching the plantacon which wee here haue begun, it fell out thus about the yeare 1627 some friends beeing togeather in Lincolnesheire, fell into some discourse about New England and the plantinge of the gospell there; and after some deliberation, we imparted our reasons by l'res [letters] & messages to some in London & the west country where it was likewise deliberately thought vppon [upon], and at length with often negociation soe ripened that in the year 1628. wee procured a patent from his Ma'tie for our planting between the Matachusetts Bay, and Charles river on the South; and the River of Merimack on the North and 3 miles on ether side of those Rivers & Bay, as allso for the government of those who did or should inhabit within that compass and the same year we sent Mr. John Endecott & some with him to beginne a plantacon & to strengthen such as he should find there which wee sent thether from Dorchester & some places adioyning [adjoining];

[1] From Dudley's letter to the Countess of London. Printed in Hart's "Source Book of American History." Dudley came over with Winthrop, and at one time was governor of the Colony.

ffrom whom the same year receivinge hopefull news.

The next year 1629 wee sent diverse shipps over w'th about 300 people, and some Cowes, Goates & Horses many of which arrived safely. Theis [these] by their too large comendacons [commendations] of the country, and the comodities thereof, invited us soe strongly to goe on that Mr. Wenthropp of Soffolke (who was well knowne in his own country & well approved heere for his pyety, liberality, wisedome & gravity) comeinge in to us, wee came to such resolution that in April 1630, wee sett saile from Old England with 4 good shipps. And in May following 8 more followed, 2 having gone before in February and March, and 2 more following in June and August, besides another set out by a private merchant. Theis 17 Shipps arrived all safe in New England, for the increase of the plantacon here theis yeare 1630. . . .

Our 4 shipps which sett out in Aprill arrived here in June and July, where wee found the colony in a sadd and unexpected condicon aboue 80 of them being dead the winter before and many of those aliue weake and sicke: all the corne & bread amongst them all hardly sufficient to feed them a fortnight, insoemuch that the remainder of 180 servants wee had the 2 years before sent over, comeinge to vs for victualls to sustaine them wee found ourselves wholly unable to feed them by reason that the p'visions [provisions] shipped for them were taken out of the shipp they were put in, and they who were trusted to shipp them in another failed us, and left them behind; whereupon necessity enforced us to our extreme loss to giue them all libertie; who had cost us about: 16 or 20 £s [sterling] a person furnishing and sending over.

But bearing theis things as wee might, wee beganne to consult of the place of our sitting downe: ffor Salem where wee landed, pleased us not. And to that purpose some were sent to the Bay[2] to search vpp the rivers for a convenient place; who vppon their returne reported to haue found a good place vppon Mistick; but some other of us seconding theis to approoue [approve] or dislike of their judgment; we found a place [that] liked vs better 3 leagues vp Charles river—And there vppon vnshipped our goods into other vessels and with much cost and labour brought them in July to Charles Towne; but there receiveing advertisements by some of the late arived shipps from London and Amsterdam of some Ffrench preparations against vs (many of our people brought with vs beeing sick of ffeavers [fevers] & the scurvy and wee thereby vnable to car[r]y vp our ordinance and baggage soe farr) wee were forced to change counsaile and for our present shelter to plant dispersedly, some at Charles Towne which standeth on the North Side of the mouth of Charles River; some on the South Side thereof, which place we named Boston (as wee intended to haue done the place wee first resolved on) some of vs vppon Mistick, which wee named Meadford; some of vs westward on Charles river, 4 miles from Charles Towne, which place wee named Watertoune; others of vs 2 miles from Boston in a place wee named Rocksbury, others vppon the river of Sawgus betweene Salem and Charles Toune. And the

[2] Boston Harbor is here referred to.

westerne men 4 miles South from Boston at a place wee named Dorchester.

This dispersion troubled some of vs, but helpe it wee could not, wanting abillity to remove to any place fit to build a Toune vppon, and the time too short to deliberate any longer least [lest] the winter should surprize vs before wee had builded our houses. . . . of the people who came over with vs from the time of their setting saile from England in Aprill 1630. vntill December followinge there dyed by estimacon about 200 at the least — Soe lowe hath the Lord brought vs! Well, yet they who survived were not discouraged but bearing God's corrections with humilitye and trusting in his mercies, and considering how after a greater ebb hee had raised vpp our neighbours at Plymouth we beganne againe in December to consult about a fitt place to build a Toune [town] vppon, leavinge all thoughts of a fort, because vppon any invasion wee were necessarily to loose our howses when we should retire thereinto; soe after diverse meetings at Boston, Rocksbury and Waterton on the 28th of December wee grew to this resolution to bind all the Assistants Mr. Endicott & Mr. Sharpe excepted, which last purposeth to returne by the next ships into England) to build howses at a place, a mile east from Waterton neere Charles river,[3] the next Springe, and to winter there the next yeare, that soe by our examples and by removeinge the ordinance and munition thether, all who were able, might be drawne thether, and such as shall come to vs hereafter to their advantage bee compelled soe to doe; and soe

[3] The place was afterward called Newtown, and is now Cambridge.

if God would, a fortifyed Toune might there grow vpp, the place fitting reasonably well thereto. . . .

But now haueing some leasure to discourse of the motiues for other mens comeinge to this place or their abstaining from it, after my brief manner I say this — That if any come hether [hither] to plant for worldly ends that canne live well at home hee co[m]mits an errour of which hee will soon repent him. But if for spirittuall [ends] and that noe particular obstacle hinder his removeall, he may finde here what may well content him: vizt: materialls to build, fewell [fuel] to burn, ground to plant, seas and rivers to ffish in, a pure ayer [air] to breath[e] in, good water to drinke till wine or beare canne be made, which togeather with the cowes, hoggs and goates brought hether allready may suffice for food, for as for foule [fowl] and venison, they are dainties here a well as in England. Ffor cloaths and beddinge they must bring them with them till time and industry produce them here. In a word, wee yett enioy [enjoy] little to bee envyed but endure much to be pittyed in the sicknes & mortalitye of our people.

HOW THE BAY COLONY DIFFERED
FROM PLYMOUTH

BY JOHN G. PALFREY [1]

The emigration of the Englishmen who settled
at Plymouth had been prompted by religious dissent. In what manner Robinson, who was capable
of speculating on political tendencies, or Brewster,
whose early position had compelled him to observe
them, had augured concerning the prospect of
public affairs in their native country, no record
tells; while the rustics of the Scrooby congregation, who fled from a government which denied
them liberty in their devotions, could have had but
little knowledge and no agency in the political
sphere. The case was widely different with the
founders of the Colony of Massachusetts Bay.
That settlement had its rise in a state of things
in England which associated religion and politics
in an intimate alliance. . . .

Winthrop, then forty-two years old, was descended from a family of good condition, long
seated at Groton, in Suffolk, where he had a
property of six or seven hundred pounds a year,
the equivalent of at least two thousand pounds
at the present day. His father was a lawyer and
magistrate. Commanding uncommon respect and
confidence from an early age, he had moved in
the circles where the highest matters of English

[1] From Palfrey's "History of New England." By permission of and by arrangement with the authorized publishers,
Houghton, Mifflin Co. Copyright, 1873.

policy were discust, by men who had been associates of Whitgift, Bacon, Essex, and Cecil. Humphrey was "a gentleman of special parts, of learning and activity, and a godly man"; in the home of his father-in-law, Thomas, third earl of Lincoln, the head in that day of the now ducal house of Newcastle, he had been the familiar companion of the patriotic nobles.

Of the assistants, Isaac Johnson, esteemed the richest of the emigrants, was another son-in-law of Lord Lincoln, and a landholder in three counties. Sir Richard Saltonstall of Halifax, in Yorkshire, was rich enough to be a bountiful contributor to the company's operations. Thomas Dudley, with a company of volunteers which he had raised, had served, thirty years before, under Henry IV of France; since which time he had managed the estates of the Earl of Lincoln. He was old enough to have lent a shrill voice to the huzzas at the defeat of the armada, and his military services had indoctrinated him in the lore of civil and religious freedom. Theophilus Eaton, an eminent London merchant, was used to courts and had been minister of Charles I in Denmark. Simon Bradstreet, the son of a Non-conformist minister in Lincolnshire, and a grandson of "a Suffolk gentleman of a fine estate," had studied at Emanuel College, Cambridge. William Vassall was an opulent West India proprietor. "The principal planters of Massachusetts," says the prejudiced Chalmers, "were English country gentlemen of no inconsiderable fortunes; of enlarged understandings, improved by liberal education; of extensive ambition, concealed under the appearance of religious humility."

120

But it is not alone from what we know of the position, character, and objects of those few members of the Massachusetts Company who were proposing to emigrate at the early period now under our notice, that we are to estimate the power and the purposes of that important corporation. It had been rapidly brought into the form which it now bore, by the political exigencies of the age. Its members had no less in hand than a wide religious and political reform—whether to be carried out in New England, or in Old England, or in both, it was for circumstances, as they should unfold themselves, to determine. The leading emigrants to Massachusetts were of that brotherhood of men who, by force of social consideration as well as of the intelligence and resolute patriotism, molded the public opinion and action of England in the first half of the seventeenth century. While the large part stayed at home to found, as it proved, the short-lived English republic, and to introduce elements into the English Constitution which had to wait another half-century for their secure reception, another part devoted themselves at once to the erection of free institutions in this distant wilderness.

In an important sense the associates of the Massachusetts Company were builders of the British, as well as of the New England, commonwealth. Some ten or twelve of them, including Cradock, the Governor, served in the Long Parliament. Of the four commoners of that Parliament distinguished by Lord Clarendon as first in influence, Vane had been governor of the company, and Hampden, Pym, and Fiennes—all patentees of Connecticut—if not members, were constantly consulted upon its affairs. The latter statement is also true of the Earl of Warwick, the Parliament's admiral, and of those excellent persons, Lord Say and Sele and Lord Brooke, both of whom at one time proposed to emigrate.

The company's meetings placed Winthrop and his colleagues in relations with numerous persons destined to act busy parts in the stirring times that were approaching—with Brereton and Hewson, afterward two of the Parliamentary major-generals; with Philip Nye, who helped Sir Henry Vane to "cozen" the Scottish Presbyterian Commissioners in the phraseology of the Solemn League and Covenant; with Samuel Vassall, whose name shares with those of Hampden and Lord Say and Sele the renown of the refusal to pay ship-money, and of courting the suit which might ruin them or emancipate England; with John Venn, who, at the head of six thousand citizens, beset the House of Lords during the trial of Lord Strafford, and whom, with three other Londoners, King Charles, after the battle of Edgehill, excluded from his offer of pardon; with Owen Rowe, the "firebrand of the city"; with Thomas Andrews, the lord mayor, who proclaimed the abolition of royalty. . . .

He who well weighs the facts which have been presented in connection with the principal emigration to Massachusetts, and other related facts which will offer themselves to notice as we proceed, may find himself conducted to the conclusion that when Winthrop and his associates prepared to convey across the water a charter from the King which, they hoped, would in their beginnings afford them some protection both from himself and through him from the powers of Continental Europe, they had conceived a project no less important than that of laying, on this side of the Atlantic, the foundations of a nation of Puritan Englishmen, foundations to be built upon as future circumstances should decide or allow. It would not perhaps be pressing the point too far to say that in view of the thick clouds that were gathering over their home, they contemplated the possibility that the time was near at hand when all that was best of what they left behind would follow them to these shores; when a renovated England, secure in freedom and pure in religion, would rise in North America; when a transatlantic English empire would fulfil, in its beneficent order, the dreams of English patriots and sages of earlier times. . . .

The *Arbella* arrived at Salem after a passage of nine weeks, and was joined in a few days by three vessels which had sailed in her company. The assistants, Ludlow and Rossiter, with a party from the west country, had landed at Nantasket a fortnight before, and some of the Leyden people, on their way to Plymouth, had reached Salem a little earlier yet. Seven vessels from Southampton made their voyages three or four weeks later. Seventeen in the whole came before winter, bringing about a thousand passengers. . . .

It is desirable to understand how this population, destined to be the germ of a state, was constituted. Of members of the Massachusetts Company, it cannot be ascertained that so many as twenty had come over. That company, as has been explained, was one formed mainly for the furtherance, not of any private interests, but of a great public object. As a corporation, it had obtained the ownership of a large American territory, on which it designed to place a colony which should be a refuge for civil and religious freedom. By combined counsels, it had arranged the method of ordering a settlement, and the liberality of its members had provided the means of transporting those who should compose it. This done, the greater portion were content to remain and await the course of events at home, while a few of their number embarked to attend to providing the asylum which very soon might be needed by them all.

The reception of the newcomers was discouraging. More than a quarter part of their predecessors at Salem had died during the previous winter, and many of the survivors were ill or feeble. The faithful Higginson was wasting with a hectic fever, which soon proved fatal. There was a scarcity of all sorts of provisions, and not corn enough for a fortnight's supply after the arrival of the fleet. "The remainder of a hundred eighty servants," who, in the two preceding years, had been conveyed over at heavy cost, were discharged from their indentures, to escape the expense of their maintenance. Sickness soon began to spread, and before the close of autumn had proved fatal to two hundred of this year's emigration. Death aims at the "shining mark" he is said to love. Lady Arbella Johnson, coming "from a paradise of plenty and pleasure, which she enjoyed in the family of a noble earldom, into a wilderness of wants," survived her arrival only a month; and her husband, esteemed and beloved by the colonists, died of grief a few weeks after. "He was a holy man and wise and died in sweet peace."

LORD BALTIMORE IN MARYLAND

(1633)

BY CONTEMPORARY WRITERS[1]

On Friday the 22 of November 1633, a small gale of winde comming gently from the Northwest, weighed from the Cowes, in the Ile of Wight, about ten in the morning; & (hauing stayed by the way twenty dayes at the Barbada's, and fourtene dayes at St. Christophers, vpon some necessary occasions,) wee arrived at Point-Comfort in Virginia, on the 24. of February following, the Lord be praised for it. At this time one Captaine Claybourne was come from parts where wee intended to plant, to Virginia, and from him wee vnderstood, that all the natiues of these parts were in preparation of defence, by reason of a rumour somebody had raised amongst them, of six ships that were come with a power of Spanyards, whose meaning was to driue all the inhabitants out of the Countrey.

[1] This account was compiled from letters written to friends in England by some of the original settlers about a year after their arrival. George Calvert, first Lord Baltimore, founder of Maryland, had sent a group of colonists to Newfoundland in 1621, but the venture being unsuccessful he secured a new grant north of the Potomac, to which, at the request of Charles I, he gave the name of Maryland, in honor of Queen Henrietta Maria. Calvert, after a visit to Virginia, returned to England and there died before his charter was actually issued. In consequence the grant was made out to Calvert's son, Cecil. Cecil Calvert at once organized

On the 3. of March wee came into Chesapeake Bay, and made sayle to the North of Patoemeck riuer, the Bay running betweene two sweete lands in the channell of 7. 8. and 9 fathome deepe, 10 leagues broad, and full of fish at the time of the yeere; It is one of the delightfullest waters I euer saw, except Potoemeck, which wee named St. Gregories. And now being in our own Countrey, wee began to giue names to places, and called the Southerne Pointe, Cape Saint Gregory; and the Northerly Point, Saint Michaels.

This riuer, of all I know, is the greatest and sweetest, much broader than the Thames; so pleasant, as I for my part, was neuer satisfied in beholding it. Few marshes or swamps, but the greatest part sollid good earth, with great Curiosity of woods which are not Choaked vp with vndershrubbes, but set commonly one from the other in such distance, as a Coach and foure horses may easily trauell through them.

At the first loaming of the ship vpon the river, wee found (as was foretold vs) all the Countrey in Armes. The King of the Paschattowayes had drawen together 1500 bowe-men, which wee ourselues saw, the woods were fired in manner of beacons the night after; and for that our vessell

a company of more than two hundred men, who effected a permanent settlement at St. Mary's, which for sixty years was the capital of the colony of Maryland, Annapolis being afterward chosen. Baltimore was not founded until 1729.

The account here given was published in London in 1634, and is the first extant description of the province. It has been conjectured that Cecil Calvert prepared it from letters written by his brothers, Leonard and George. The account is believed to preserve the exact language of the original writers of the letters. Printed in "Old South Leaflets."

was the greatest that euer those Indians saw, the scowtes reported wee came in a Canoe, as bigge as an Island, and had as many men as there bee trees in the woods.

Wee sayled vp the river till wee came to Heron Ilands, so called from the infinite swarmes of that fowle there. The first of those Ilands we called Saint Clement's: The second Saint Katharine's; And the third, Saint Cicilie's. We took land first in Saint Clement's, which is compassed about with a shallow water, and admitts no accesse without wading; here by the ouerturning of the Shallop, the maids which had been washing at the land were almost drowned, beside the losse of much linnen, and amongst the rest, I lost the best of mine which is a very maine losse in these parts. The ground is couered thicke with pokickeries (which is a wild Wall-nut very hard and thick of shell; but the meate (though little) is passing sweete,) with black Wall-nuts, and acorns bigger than Ours. It abounds with Vines and Salletts, hearbs and flowers, full of Cedar and Sassafras. It is but 400 acres bigg, & therefore too little for vs to settle vpon.

Heere we went to a place, where a large tree was made into a Crosse; and taking it on our shoulders, wee carried it to the place appointed for it. The Gouernour and Commissioners putting their hands first vnto it, then the rest of the chiefest aduenturers. At the place prepared wee all kneeled downe, & said certain Prayers; taking possession of the Countrey for our Saviour, and for our soueraigne Lord the King of England. . . .

The Gouernour being returned, wee Came some nine leagues lower to a riuer on the North Side of that land, as bigg as the Thames: which wee called Saint Gregorie's river.[2] It runs vp to the North about 20 miles before it comes to the fresh. This river makes two excellent Bayes, for 300 sayle of Shippes of 1000. tunne, to harbour in with great safety. The one Bay we named Saint George's; the other (and more inward) Saint Marie's. The King of Yaocomico, dwells on the left-hand or side thereof: & we tooke vp our Seate on the right, one mile within the land. It is as braue a piece of ground to set down on as most is in the Countrey, & I suppose as good, (if not much better) than the primest parcel of English ground.

Our Town we call Saint Marie's; and to auoid all iust occasion of offence, & collour of wrong, wee bought of the King for Hatchets, Axes, Howes, and Cloathes, a quantitie of some 30 miles of Land, which wee call Augusta Carolina; And that which made them the more willing to sell it, was the warres they had with the Sasqusa-hanoughs,[3] a mighty bordering nation, who came often into their Countrey, to waste & destroy; & forced many of them to leaue their Countrey, and passe ouer Patoemeck to free themselues from perill before wee came. God no doubt disposing all this for them, who were to bring his law and light among the Infidells. Yet, seeing wee came soe well prepared with armes, their feare was much lesse, & they could be content to dwell by vs: Yet doe they daily relinquish their houses, lands, & Cornefields, & leaue them to vs. Is not this a piece of wonder that a nation, which a few dayes before

[2] Now called the Susquehanna.

[3] The Susquehanna Indians.

was in armes with the rest against vs, should yeeld themselues now vnto vs like lambes, & giue vs their houses, land & linings, for a trifle? *Digitus Dei est hic:* and surely some great good is entended by God to his Nation. Some few families of Indians, are permitted to stay by vs till next yeere, & then the land is free. . . .

And now to returne to the place itselfe, chosen for our plantation. Wee haue been vpon it but one month, and therefore can make no large relation of it. Yet thus much I can say of it allready; For our own safety, we haue built a good strong Fort or Palizado, & haue mounted vpon it one good piece of Ordnance, and 4 Murderers, and haue seuen pieces of Ordnance more, ready to mount forthwith. For our prouision, heere is some store of Peasen, and Beanes, and Wheate left on the ground by the Indians, who had satisfaction for it.

Wee haue planted since wee came, as much Maize (or Indian Wheate) as will suffice (if God prosper it) much more company than we haue. It is vp about knee high aboue ground allready, and wee expect return of 1000. for one, as wee haue reason for our hope, from the experience of the yeelde in other parts of this Countrey, as is very credibly related to vs.

Wee haue also English Peasen, & French-beanes, Cotten, Oringes, Limons, Melocotunes, Apples, Peares, Potatos, and Sugar-Canes of our owne planting, beside Hortage comming vp very finely.

But such is the quantity of Vines and Grapes now allready vpon them (though young) as I dare say if wee had Vessells and skill, wee might make many a tonne of Wine, euen from about our Plantation; and such Wine, as those of Virginia say (for yet we can say nothing) as is as good as the Wine of Spaine. I feare they exceede; but surely very good. For the Clime of this Countrey is neere the same with Sivill and Corduba: lying betweene 38 & 40 degrees of Northerlie latitude.

Of Hoggs wee haue allready got from Achomack (a plantation in Virginia) to the number of 100, & more: and some 30 Cowes; and more wee expect daily, with Goates and Hennes; our Horses and Sheepe wee must have out of England, or some other place by the way, for wee can haue none in Virginia.

ROGER WILLIAMS IN RHODE ISLAND

(1636)

BY NATHANIEL MORTON[1]

In the year 1634 Mr. Roger Williams removed from Plymouth to Salem: he had lived about three years at Plymouth, where he was well accepted as an assistant in the ministry to Mr. Ralph Smith, then pastor of the church there, but by degrees venting of divers of his own singular opinions, and seeking to impose them upon others, he not finding such a concurrence as he expected, he desired his dismission to the Church of Salem, which though some were unwilling to, yet through the prudent counsel of Mr. Brewster (the ruling elder there) fearing that his continuance amongst them might cause division, and [thinking that] there being then many able men in the Bay, they would better deal with him then [than] themselves could . . . the Church of Plymouth consented to his dismission, and such as did adhere to him were also dismissed, and removed with him, or not long after him, to Salem. . . .

---

[1] From Morton's "New England Memorial," published at the request of the Commissioners of the Four United Colonies of New England. Morton lived in the family of Governor Bradford and served as secretary of the court at Plymouth. This fact should be kept in mind when reading his account.

But he having in one year's time filled that place
with principles of rigid separation, and tending to
Anabaptistry, the prudent Magistrates of the
Massachusetts Jurisdiction, sent to the Church of
Salem, desiring them to forbear calling him to
office, which they not hearkening to, was a cause
of much disturbance; for Mr. Williams had begun,
and then being in office, he proceeded more vigorously to vent many dangerous opinions, as amongst
many others these were some; That it is not lawful for an unregenerate man to pray, nor to take
an Oath, and in special, not the Oath of Fidelity
to the Civil Government; nor was it lawful for a
godly man to have communion either in Family
Prayer, or in an Oath with such as they judged
unregenerate: and therefore he himself refused the
Oath of Fidelity, and taught others so to do; also,
That it was not lawful so much as to hear the
godly Ministers of England, when any occasionally
went thither; & therefore he admonished any
Church-members that had done so, as for hainous
sin: also he spake dangerous words against the
Patent, which was the foundation of the Government of the Massachusets Colony: also he affirmed, That the Magistrates had nothing to do in
matters of the first Table [of the commandments],
but only the second; and that there should be a
general and unlimited Toleration of all Religions,
and for any man to be punished for any matters
of his Conscience, was persecution. . . .
He persisted, and grew more violent in his
way, insomuch as he staying at home in his own
house, sent a Letter, which was delivered and read
in the publick Church assembly, the scope of which
was to give them notice, That if the Church of

Salem would not separate not only from the Churches of Old-England, but the Churches of New-England too, he would separate from them: the more prudent and sober part of the Church being amazed at his way, could not yield unto him: whereupon he never came to the Church Assembly more, professing separation from them as Antichristian, and not only so, but he withdrew all private religious Communion from any that would hold Communion with the Church there, insomuch as he would not pray nor give thanks at meals with his own wife nor any of his family, because they went to the Church Assemblies . . . which the prudent Magistrates understanding, and seeing things grow more and more towards a general division and disturbance, after all other means used in vain, they passed a sentence of Banishment against him out of the Massachusets Colony, as against a disturber of the peace, both of the Church and Commonwealth.

After which Mr. Williams sat down in a place called Providence, out of the Massachusets Jurisdiction, and was followed by many of the members of the Church of Salem, who did zealously adhere to him, and who cried out of the Persecution that was against him: some others also resorted to him from other parts. They had not been long there together, but from rigid separation they fell to Anabaptistry, renouncing the Baptism which they had received in their Infancy, and taking up another Baptism, and so began a Church in that way; but Mr. Williams stopt not there long, for after some time he told the people that had followed him, and joyned with him in a new Baptism, that he was out of the way himself, and had mis-led them, for he did not finde that there was any upon earth that could administer Baptism, and therefore their last Baptism was a nullity, as well as their first; and therefore they must lay down all, and wait for the coming of new Apostles: and so they dissolved themselves, and turned Seekers, keeping that one Principle, That every one should have liberty to Worship God according to the Light of their own Consciences; but otherwise not owning any Churches or Ordinances of God any where upon Earth.

THE FOUNDING OF CONNECTICUT

(1633—1636)

BY ALEXANDER JOHNSTON[1]

During the ten years after 1620, the twin colonies of Plymouth and Massachusetts Bay had been fairly shaken down into their places, and had even begun to look around them for opportunities of extension. It was not possible that the fertile and inviting territory to the southwest should long escape their notice. In 1629, De Rasières, an envoy from New Amsterdam, was at Plymouth. He found the Plymouth people building a shallop for the purpose of obtaining a share in the wampum trade of Narragansett Bay; and he very shrewdly sold them at a bargain enough wampum to supply their needs, for fear they should discover at Narragansett the more profitable peltry trade beyond. This artifice only put off the evil day.

Within the next three years, several Plymouth men, including Winslow, visited the Connecticut River, "not without profit." In April, 1631, a Connecticut Indian visited Governor Winthrop at Boston, asking for settlers, and offering to find them corn and furnish eighty beaver skins a year. Winthrop declined even to send an exploring

---

[1] From Johnston's "History of Connecticut." By permission of, and by arrangement with, the authorized publishers, Houghton, Mifflin Co. Copyright, 1887, by Alexander Johnston.

party. In the midsummer of 1633, Winslow went to Boston to propose a joint occupation of the new territory by Plymouth and Massachusetts Bay; but the latter still refused, doubting the profit and the safety of the venture.

Three months later Plymouth undertook the work alone. A small vessel, under command of William Holmes, was sent around by sea to the mouth of the Connecticut River, with the frame of a trading house and workmen to put it up. When Holmes had sailed up the river as far as the place where Hartford was afterward built, he found the Dutch already in possession. For ten years they had been talking of erecting a fort on the Varsche River; but the ominous and repeated appearance of New Englanders in the territory had roused them to action at last.

John Van Corlear, with a few men, had been commissioned by Governor Van Twiller, and had put up a rude earthwork, with two guns, within the present jurisdiction of Hartford. His summons to Holmes to stop under penalty of being fired into met with no more respect than was shown by the commandant of Rensselaerswyck to his challengers, according to the veracious Knickerbocker. Holmes declared that he had been sent up the river, and was going up the river, and furthermore he went up the river. His little vessel passed on to the present site of Windsor. Here the crew disembarked, put up and garrisoned their trading house, and then returned home. Plymouth had at least planted the flag far within the coveted and disputed territory.

In December of the following year a Dutch force of seventy men from New Amsterdam appeared before the trading house to drive out the intruders. He must be strong who drives a Yankee away from a profitable trade; and the attitude of the little garrison was so determined that the Dutchmen, after a few hostile demonstrations, decided that the nut was too hard to crack, and withdrew. For about twenty years thereafter the Dutch held post at Hartford, isolated from Dutch support by a continually deepening mass of New Englanders, who refrained from hostilities, and waited until the apple was ripe enough to drop.

With respect to the claims of the Indians, the attitudes of the two parties to the struggle were directly opposite. The Dutch came on the strength of purchase from the Pequots, the conquerors and lords paramount of the local Indians. Holmes brought to the Connecticut River in his vessel the local sachems, who had been driven away by the Pequots, and made his purchases from them. The English policy will account for the unfriendly disposition of the Pequots, and, when followed up by the tremendous overthrow of the Pequots, for Connecticut's permanent exemption from Indian difficulties. The Connecticut settlers followed a straight road, buying lands fairly from the Indians found in possession, ignoring those who claimed a supremacy based on violence, and, in case of resistance by the latter, asserting and maintaining for Connecticut an exactly similar title,—the right of the stronger. Those who claimed right received it; those who preferred force were accommodated.

One route to the new territory by Long Island Sound and the Connecticut River, had thus been appropriated. The other, the overland route through Massachusetts, was explored during the same year, 1633, by one John Oldham, who was murdered by the Pequots two years afterward. He found his way westward to the Connecticut River, and brought back most appetizing accounts of the upper Connecticut Valley; and his reports seem to have suggested a way out of a serious difficulty which had come to a head in Massachusetts Bay.

The colony of Massachusetts Bay was at this time limited to a district covering not more than twenty or thirty miles from the sea, and its greatest poverty, as Cotton stated, was a poverty of men. And yet the colony was to lose part of its scanty store of men. Three of the eight Massachusetts towns, Dorchester, Watertown, and Newtown (now Cambridge), had been at odds with the other five towns on several occasions; and the assigned reasons are apparently so frivolous as to lead to the suspicion that some fundamental difference was at the bottom of them. The three towns named had been part of the great Puritan influx of 1630. Their inhabitants were "newcomers," and this slight division may have been increased by the arrival and settlement, in 1633, of a number of strong men at these three towns, notably Hooker, Stone, and Haynes at Newtown. Dorchester, Watertown, and Newtown showed many symptoms of an increase of local feeling: the two former led the way, in October, 1633, in establishing town governments under "selectmen;" and all three neglected or evaded, more or less, the fundamental feature of Massachusetts policy,—the limitation of office-holding and the elective franchise to church-members. The three towns fell into the position of the commonwealth's opposition, a position not particularly desirable at the time and under all the circumstances.

The ecclesiastical leaders of Dorchester were Warham and Maverick; of Newtown, Hooker and Stone; of Watertown, Phillips. Haynes of Newtown, Ludlow of Dorchester, and Pynchon of Roxbury, were the principal lay leaders of the half-formed opposition. Some have thought that Haynes was jealous of Governor Winthrop, Hooker of Cotton, and Ludlow of everybody. But the opposition, if it can be fairly called an opposition, was not so definite as to be traceable to any such personal source. The strength which marked the divergence was due neither to ambition nor to jealousy, but to the strength of mind and character which marked the leaders of the minority.

Thomas Hooker and Samuel Stone were of Emmanuel College, Cambridge. Hooker began to preach at Chelmsford in 1626, and was silenced for non-conformity in 1629. He then taught school, his assistant being John Eliot, afterward the apostle to the Indians; but the chase after him became warmer, and in 1630 he retired to Holland and resumed his preaching. In 1632 he and Stone came to New England as pastor and teacher of the church at Newtown; and the two took part in the migration to Hartford. Here Hooker became the undisputed ecclesiastical leader of Connecticut until his death in 1647. John Warham and John Maverick, both of Exeter in England, came to New England in 1630, as pastor and teacher of Dorchester. Maverick died while preparing to follow his church, but Warham settled with his parishioners at Windsor, and died there in 1670. George Phillips, also a Cambridge

man, came to New England in 1630, as pastor of
the church at Watertown. He took no part in
the migration, but lived and died at Watertown.
Fate seems to have determined that Wendell Phillips should belong to Massachusetts.

Roger Ludlow was Endicott's brother-in-law.
He came to New England in 1630, and settled at
Dorchester. He was deputy governor in 1634,
and seems to have been "slated," to use the modern term, for the governorship in the following
year. But this private agreement among the deputies was broken, for some unknown reason, by the
voters, who chose Haynes, perhaps as a less objectionable representative of the opposition. Ludlow
complained so openly and angrily of the failure
to carry out the agreement that he was dropped
from the magistracy at the next election. He went
at once to Connecticut, and was deputy governor
there in alternate years until 1654. Incensed at
the interference of New Haven to prevent his
county, Fairfield, from waging an independent
warfare against the Dutch, he went to Virginia
in 1654, taking the records of the county with him.
It is not known when or where he died. Pynchon,
the third lay leader of the opposition, took part in
the migration, but remained within the jurisdiction of Massachusetts, founding the town of
Springfield.

At the May session of the Massachusetts General Court in 1634, an application for "liberty to
remove" was received from Newtown. It was
granted. At the September session the request
was changed into one for removal to Connecticut.
This was a very different matter, and, after long
debate, was defeated by the vote of the Assist-

ants, tho the Deputies passed it. Various reasons were assigned for the request to remove to Connecticut,—lack of room in their present locations, the desire to save Connecticut from the Dutch, and "the strong bent of their spirits to remove thither;" but the last looks like the strongest reason. In like manner, while the arguments to the contrary were those which would naturally suggest themselves, the weakening of Massachusetts, and the peril of the emigrants, the concluding argument, that "the removing of a candlestick" would be "a great judgment," seems to show the feeling of all parties that the secession was the result of discord between two parties.

Haynes was made governor at the next General Court. Successful inducements were offered to some of the Newtown people to remove to Boston, and some few concessions were made. But the migration which had been denied to the corporate towns had probably been begun by individuals. There is a tradition that some of the Watertown people passed this winter of 1634-35 at the place where Wethersfield now stands. In May, 1635, the Massachusetts General Court voted that liberty be granted to the people of Watertown and Roxbury to remove themselves to any place within the jurisdiction of Massachusetts. In March, 1636, the secession having already been accomplished, the General Court issued a "Commission to Several Persons to govern the people at Connecticut."

Its preamble reads: "Whereas, upon some reasons and grounds, there are to remove from this our Commonwealth and body of the Massachusetts in America divers of our loving friends and neighbors, freemen and members of Newtown,

Dorchester, Watertown, and other places, who are resolved to transport themselves and their estates unto the river of Connecticut, there to reside and inhabit; and to that end divers are there already, and divers others shortly to go." This tacit permission was the only authorization given by Massachusetts; but it should be noted that the unwilling permission was made more gracious by a kindly loan of cannon and ammunition for the protection of the new settlements.

If it be true that some of the Watertown people had wintered at Wethersfield in 1634-35, this was the first civil settlement in Connecticut; and it is certain that, all through the following spring, summer, and autumn, detached parties of Watertown people were settling at Wethersfield. During the summer of 1635, a Dorchester party appeared near the Plymouth factory, and laid the foundations of the town of Windsor. In October of the same year a party of sixty persons, including women and children, largely from Newtown, made the overland march and settled where Hartford now stands. Their journey was begun so late that the winter overtook them before they reached the river, and, as they had brought their cattle with them, they found great difficulty in getting everything across the river by means of rafts.

It may have been that the echoes of all these preparations had reached England, and stirred the tardy patentees to action. During the autumn of 1635, John Winthrop, Jr., agent of the Say and Sele associates, reached Boston, with authority to build a large fort at the mouth of the Connecticut River. He was to be "Governor of the River

Connecticut" for one year, and he at once issued a proclamation to the Massachusetts emigrants, asking "under what right and preference they had lately taken up their plantation."

It is said that they agreed to give up any lands demanded by him, or to return on having their expenses repaid. A more dangerous influence, however, soon claimed Winthrop's attention. Before the winter set in he had sent a party to seize the designated spot for a fort at the mouth of the Connecticut River. His promptness was needed. Just as his men had thrown up a work sufficient for defense and had mounted a few guns, a Dutch ship from New Amsterdam appeared, bringing a force intended to appropriate the same place. Again the Dutch found themselves a trifle late; and their post at Hartford was thus finally cut off from effective support.

This was a horrible winter to the advanced guard of English settlers on the upper Connecticut. The navigation of the river was completely blocked by ice before the middle of November; and the vessels which were to have brought their winter supplies by way of Long Island Sound and the river were forced to return to Boston, leaving the wretched settlers unprovided for. For a little while some scanty supplies of corn were obtained from the neighboring Indians, but this resource soon failed. About seventy persons straggled down the river to the fort at its mouth. There they found and dug out of the ice a sixty-ton vessel, and made their way back to Boston. Others turned back on the way they had come, and struggled through the snow and ice to "the Bay." But a few held their grip on the new territory. Subsisting first on a little corn bought from more distant Indians, then by hunting, and finally on ground-nuts and acorns dug from under the snow, they fought through the winter and held their ground. But it was a narrow escape. Spring found them almost exhausted, their unsheltered cattle dead, and just time enough to bring necessary supplies from home. The Dorchester people alone lost cattle to the value of two thousand pounds.

The Newtown congregation, in October, 1635, found customers for their old homes in a new party from England; and in the following June Hooker and Stone led their people overland to Connecticut. They numbered one hundred, with one hundred and sixty head of cattle. Women and children were of the party. Mrs. Hooker, who was ill, was carried on a litter; and the journey, of "about one hundred miles," occupied two weeks. Its termination was well calculated to dissipate the evil auguries of the previous winter. The Connecticut Valley in early June! Its green meadows, flanked by wooded hills, lay before them. Its oaks, whose patriarch was to shelter their charter, its great elms and tulip-trees, were broken by the silver ribbon of the river; here and there were the wigwams of the Indians, or the cabins of the survivors of the winter; and, over and through all, the light of a day in June welcomed the newcomers. The thought of abandoning Connecticut disappeared forever.

WITCHCRAFT IN NEW ENGLAND

(1647—1696)

BY JOHN G. PALFREY [1]

The people of Massachusetts in the seventeenth century, like all other Christian people at that time and later,—at least, with extremely rare individual exceptions,—believed in the reality of a hideous crime called witchcraft. They thought they had Scripture for that belief, and they knew they had law for it, explicit and abundant; and with them law and Scripture were absolute authorities for the regulation of opinion and of conduct.

In a few instances, witches were believed to have appeared in the earlier years of New England. But the cases had been sporadic. The first instance of an execution for witchcraft is said to have occurred in Connecticut, soon after the settlement [1647, May 30th]; but the circumstances are not known, and the fact has been doubted. A year later, one Margaret Jones, of Charlestown in Massachusetts, and it has been said, two other women in Dorchester and Cambridge, were convicted and executed for the goblin crime. These cases appear to have excited no more attention than would have been given to the commission of any

[1] From Palfrey's "History of New England." By permission of, and by arrangement with, the authorized publishers, Houghton, Mifflin Co. Copyright, 1873.

other felony, and no judicial record of them survives. . . .

With three or four exceptions,—for the evidence respecting the asserted sufferers at Dorchester and Cambridge is imperfect,—no person appears to have been punished for witchcraft in Massachusetts, nor convicted of it, for more than sixty years after the settlement, though there had been three or four trials of other persons suspected of the crime. At the time when the question respecting the colonial charter was rapidly approaching an issue, and the public mind was in feverish agitation, the ministers sent out a paper of proposals for collecting facts concerning witchcraft [1681]. This brought out a work from President Mather entitled "Illustrious Providences," in which that influential person related numerous stories of the performances of persons leagued with the Devil [1684].

The imagination of his restless young son[2] was stimulated, and circumstances fed the flame. In the last year of the government of Andros [1688], a daughter, thirteen years old, of John Goodwin,—a mason living at the South End of Boston,—had a quarrel with an Irish washerwoman about some missing clothes. The woman's mother took it up, and scolded provokingly. Thereupon the wicked child, profiting, as it seems, by what she had been hearing and reading on the mysterious subject, "cried out upon her," as the phrase was, as a witch, and proceeded to act the part understood to be fit for a bewitched person; in which behavior she was presently joined by three others of the

[2] Cotton Mather, son of Increase Mather, the president of Harvard College.

circle, one of them only four or five years old. Now they would lose their hearing, now their sight, now their speech; and sometimes all three faculties at once. They mewed like kittens; they barked like dogs.

Cotton Mather prayed with one of them; but she lost her hearing, he says, when he began, and recovered it as soon as he finished. Four Boston ministers and one of Charlestown held a meeting, and passed a day in fasting and prayer, by which exorcism the youngest imp was "delivered." The poor woman, crazed with all this pother,—if in her right mind before,—and defending herself unskilfully in her foreign gibberish and with the volubility of her race, was interpreted as making some confession. A gossiping witness testified that six years before she had heard another woman say that she had seen the accused come down a chimney. She was required to repeat the Lord's Prayer in English,—an approved test; but being a Catholic, she had never learned it in that language. She could recite it, after a fashion, in Latin; but she was no scholar, and made some mistakes. The helpless wretch was convicted and sent to the gallows.

Cotton Mather took the oldest "afflicted" girl to his house, where she dexterously played upon his self-conceit to stimulate his credulity. She satisfied him that Satan regarded him as his most terrible enemy, and avoided him with especial awe. When he prayed or read in the Bible, she was seized with convulsion fits. When he called to family devotion she would whistle, and sing, and scream, and pretend to try to strike and kick him; but her blows would be stopt before reaching his body, indicating that he was unassailable by the Evil One. Mather published an account of these transactions,[3] with a collection of other appropriate matter. The treatise circulated not only in Massachusetts, but widely also in England, where it obtained the warm commendation of Richard Baxter; and it may be supposed to have had an important effect in producing the more disastrous delusion which followed three years after. The Goodwin children soon got well: in other words, they were tired of their atrocious foolery; and the death of their victim gave them a pretense for a return to decent behavior. . . .

Martha Corey and Rebecca Nourse were cried out against. Both were church-members of excellent character; the latter seventy years of age. They were examined by the same magistrates, and sent to prison, and with them a child of Sarah Good, only four or five years old, also charged with diabolical practises. Mr. Parris preached upon the text, "Have not I chosen you twelve, and one of you is a devil?" Sarah Cloyse, understanding the allusion to be to Nourse, who was her sister, went out of church, and was accordingly cried out upon, examined, and committed. Elizabeth Procter was another person charged. The Deputy-Governor and five magistrates came to Salem for the examination of the two prisoners last named. Procter appealed to one of the children who was accusing her. "Dear child," she said, "it is not so; there is another judgment, dear child:" and presently they denounced as a witch her husband, who stood by her side. A week afterward war-

---

[3] This work was entitled "Wonders of the Invisible World." It is now much sought after by collectors of Americana.

rants were issued for the apprehension of four other suspected persons; and a few days later for three others, one of whom, Philip English, was the principal merchant of Salem. On the same day, on the information of one of the possessed girls, an order was sent to Maine for the arrest of George Burroughs, formerly a candidate for the ministry at Salem Village, and now minister of Wells. The witness said that Burroughs, besides being a wizard, had killed his first two wives, and other persons whose ghosts had appeared to her and denounced him. . . .

Affairs were in this condition when the King's Governor arrived. About a hundred alleged witches were now in jail, awaiting trial. Their case was one of the first matters to which his attention was called. Without authority for so doing,—for by the charter which he represented, the establishment of judicial courts was a function of the General Court,—he proceeded to institute a special commission of Oyer and Terminer, consisting of seven magistrates, first of whom was the hard, obstinate, narrow-minded Stoughton. The commissioners applied themselves to their office without delay. Their first act was to try Bridget Bishop, against whom an accusation twenty years old, and retracted by its author on his death-bed, had been revived. The court sentenced her to die by hanging, and she was accordingly hanged at the end of eight days. Cotton Mather, in his account of the proceedings, relates that as she passed along the street under guard, Bishop "had given a look toward the great and spacious meeting-house of Salem, and immediately a dæmon, invisibly entering the house, tore down a part of it." It may be guessed that a plank or a partition had given way under the pressure of the crowd of lookers-on collected for so extraordinary a spectacle.

At the end of another four weeks the court sat again and sentenced five women, two of Salem, and one each of Amesbury, Ipswich, and Topsfield, all of whom were executed, protesting their innocence. In respect to one of them, Rebecca Nourse, a matron eminent for piety and goodness, a verdict of acquittal was first rendered. But Stoughton sent the jury out again, reminding them that in her examination, in reference to certain witnesses against her who had confest their own guilt, she had used the expression, "they came among us." Nourse was deaf, and did not catch what had been going on. When it was afterward repeated to her she said that by the coming among us she meant that they had been in prison together. But the jury adopted the court's interpretation of the word as signifying an acknowledgment that they had met at a witch orgy. The Governor was disposed to grant her a pardon. But Parris, who had an ancient grudge against her, interfered and prevailed. On the last communion day before her execution she was taken into church, and formally excommunicated by Noyes, her minister. . . .

In the course of the next month, in which the Governor left Boston for a short tour of inspection in the Eastern country, fifteen persons—six women in one day, and on another eight women and one man—were tried, convicted, and sentenced. Eight of them were hanged. The brave Giles Corey, eighty years of age, being arraigned, refused to plead. He said that the whole thing was an imposture, and that it was of no use to put himself on his trial, for every trial had ended in a conviction,—which was the fact. It is shocking to relate that, suffering the penalty of the English common law for a contumacious refusal to answer,—the *peine forte et dure*,—he was prest to death with heavy weights laid on his body. By not pleading he intended to protect the inheritance of his children, which, as he had been informed, would by a conviction of felony have been forfeit to the crown.

There had been twenty human victims, Corey included; besides two dogs, their accomplices in the mysterious crime. Fifty persons had obtained a pardon by confessing; a hundred and fifty were in prison awaiting trial; and charges had been made against two hundred more. The accusers were now flying at high quarries. Hezekiah Usher, known to the reader as an ancient magistrate of fair consideration, was complained of; and Mrs. Thacher, mother-in-law of Corwin, the justice who had taken the earliest examinations. Zeal in pushing forward the prosecution began to seem dangerous; for what was to prevent an accused person from securing himself by confession, and then revenging himself on the accuser by arraigning him as a former ally? . . .

The drunken fever-fit was now over, and with returning sobriety came profound contrition and disgust. A few still held out against the return of reason. There are some men who never own that they have been in the wrong, and a few men who are forever incapable of seeing it. Stoughton, with his bull-dog stubbornness, that might in other times have made him a St. Dominic, continued to insist that the business had been all right, and that the only mistake was in putting a stop to it. Cotton Mather was always infallible in his own eyes. In the year after the executions he had the satisfaction of studying another remarkable case of possession in Boston; but when it and the treatise which he wrote upon it failed to excite much attention, and it was plain that the tide had set the other way, he soon got his consent to let it run at its own pleasure, and turned his excursive activity to other objects. . . .

Members of some of the juries, in a written public declaration, acknowledged the fault of their wrongful verdicts, entreated forgiveness, and protested that, "according to their present minds, they would none of them do such things again, on such grounds, for the whole world; praying that this act of theirs might be accepted in way of satisfaction for their offense." A day of General Fasting was proclaimed by authority, to be observed throughout the jurisdiction, in which the people were invited to pray that "whatever mistakes on either hand had been fallen into, either by the body of this people, or by any orders of men, referring to the late tragedy raised among us by Satan and his instruments, through the awful judgment of God, he would humble them therefor, and pardon all the errors of his servants and people."

THE ENGLISH CONQUEST OF NEW YORK

(1664)

BY JOHN R. BRODHEAD[1]

England now determined boldly to rob Holland
of her American province. King Charles II accordingly sealed a patent granting to the Duke
of York and Albany a large territory in America,
comprehending Long Island and the islands in its
neighborhood—his title to which Lord Stirling
had released—and all the lands and rivers from
the west side of the Connecticut River to the east
side of Delaware Bay. This sweeping grant included the whole of New Netherlands and a part
of the territory of Connecticut, which, two years
before, Charles had confirmed to Winthrop and his
associates.

The Duke of York lost no time in giving effect
to his patent. As lord high admiral he directed
the fleet. Four ships, the *Guinea,* of thirty-six
guns; the *Elias,* of thirty; the *Martin,* of sixteen; and the *William and Nicholas,* of ten, were
detached for service against New Netherlands, and
about four hundred fifty regular soldiers, with
their officers, were embarked. The command of
the expedition was intrusted to Colonel Richard
Nicolls, a faithful Royalist, who had served under
Turenne with James, and had been made one of

[1] From Brodhead's "History of New York."

the gentlemen of his bedchamber. Nicolls was also appointed to be the Duke's deputy-governor, after the Dutch possessions should have been reduced.

With Nicolls were associated Sir Robert Carr, Colonel George Cartwright, and Samuel Maverick, as royal commissioners to visit the several colonies in New England. These commissioners were furnished with detailed instructions; and the New England governments were required by royal letters to "join and assist them vigorously" in reducing the Dutch to subjection. A month after the departure of the squadron the Duke of York conveyed to Lord Berkeley and Sir George Carteret all the territory between the Hudson and Delaware Rivers, from Cape May north to 41° 40′ latitude, and thence to the Hudson, in 41° latitude, "hereafter to be called by the name or names of Nova Cæsarea or New Jersey."

Intelligence from Boston that an English expedition against New Netherlands had sailed from Portsmouth was soon communicated to Stuyvesant by Captain Thomas Willett; and the burgomasters and *schepens* of New Amsterdam were summoned to assist the council with their advice. The capital was ordered to be put in a state of defense, guards to be maintained, and *schippers* to be warned. As there was very little powder at Fort Amsterdam a supply was demanded from New Amstel, and a loan of five or six thousand guilders was asked from Rensselaerswyck. The ships about to sail for Curaçao were stopt; agents were sent to purchase provisions at New Haven; and as the enemy was expected to approach through Long Island Sound, spies were sent to obtain intelligence at West Chester and Milford.

But at the moment when no precaution should have been relaxed, a dispatch from the West India directors, who appear to have been misled by advices from London, announced that no danger need be apprehended from the English expedition, as it was sent out by the King only to settle the affairs of his colonies and establish episcopacy, which would rather benefit the company's interests in New Netherlands. Willett now retracting his previous statements, a perilous confidence returned. The Curaçao ships were allowed to sail; and Stuyvesant, yielded to the solicitation of his council, went up the river to look after affairs at Fort Orange.

The English squadron had been ordered to assemble at Gardiner's Island. But, parting company in a fog, the *Guinea*, with Nicolls and Cartwright on board, made Cape Cod, and went on to Boston, while the other ships put in at Piscataway. The commissioners immediately demanded the assistance of Massachusetts, but the people of the Bay, who feared, perhaps, that the King's success in reducing the Dutch would enable him the better to put down his enemies in New England, were full of excuses. Connecticut, however, showed sufficient alacrity; and Winthrop was desired to meet the squadron at the west end of Long Island, whither it would sail with the first fair wind.

When the truth of Willett's intelligence became confirmed, the council sent an express to recall Stuyvesant from Fort Orange. Hurrying back to the capital, the anxious director endeavored to redeem the time which had been lost. The municipal authorities ordered one-third of the inhabitants, without exception, to labor every third day at the fortifications; organized a permanent guard; forbade the brewers to malt any grain; and called on the provincial government for artillery and ammunition. Six pieces, besides the fourteen previously allotted, and a thousand pounds of powder were accordingly granted to the city. The colonists around Fort Orange, pleading their own danger from the savages, could afford no help; but the soldiers of Esopus were ordered to come down, after leaving a small garrison at Ronduit.

In the meantime the English squadron had anchored just below the Narrows, in Nyack Bay, between New Utrecht and Coney Island. The mouth of the river was shut up; communication between Long Island and Manhattan, Bergen and Achter Cul, interrupted; several yachts on their way to the South River captured; and the blockhouse on the opposite shore of Staten Island seized. Stuyvesant now dispatched Counsellor de Decker, Burgomaster Van der Grist, and the two domines Megapolensis with a letter to the English commanders inquiring why they had come, and why they continued at Nyack without giving notice. The next morning, which was Saturday, Nicolls sent Colonel Cartwright, Captain Needham, Captain Groves, and Mr. Thomas Delavall up to Fort Amsterdam with a summons for the surrender of "the town situate on the island and commonly known by the name of Manhatoes, with all the forts thereunto belonging."

This summons was accompanied by a proclamation declaring that all who would submit to his majesty's government should be protected "in his majesty's laws and justice," and peaceably enjoy their property. Stuyvesant immediately called together the council and the burgomasters, but would not allow the terms offered by Nicolls to be communicated to the people, lest they might insist on capitulating. In a short time several of the burghers and city officers assembled at the Stadt-Huys. It was determined to prevent the enemy from surprizing the town; but, as opinion was generally against protracted resistance, a copy of the English communication was asked from the director. On the following Monday the burgomasters explained to a meeting of the citizens the terms offered by Nicolls. But this would not suffice; a copy of the paper itself must be exhibited. Stuyvesant then went in person to the meeting. "Such a course," said he, "would be disapproved of in the Fatherland—it would discourage the people." All his efforts, however, were in vain; and the director, protesting that he should not be held answerable for the "calamitous consequences," was obliged to yield to the popular will.

Nicolls now addrest a letter to Winthrop, who with other commissioners from New England had joined the squadron, authorizing him to assure Stuyvesant that, if Manhattan should be delivered up to the King, "any people from the Netherlands may freely come and plant there or thereabouts; and such vessels of their own country may freely come thither, and any of them may as freely return home in vessels of their own country." Visiting the city under a flag of truce Winthrop delivered this to Stuyvesant outside the fort and urged him to surrender. The director declined; and, returning to the fort, he opened Nicolls' letter before the council and the burgomasters, who desired that it should be communicated, as "all which regarded the public welfare ought to be made public." Against this Stuyvesant earnestly remonstrated, and, finding that the burgomasters continued firm, in a fit of passion he "tore the letter in pieces." The citizens suddenly ceasing their work at the palisades, hurried to the Stadt-Huys, and sent three of their number to the fort to demand the letter.

In vain the director hastened to pacify the burghers and urge them to go on with the fortifications. "Complaints and curses" were uttered on all sides against the company's misgovernment; resistance was declared to be idle; "The letter! the letter!" was the general cry. To avoid a mutiny Stuyvesant yielded, and a copy, made out from the collected fragments, was handed to the burgomasters. In answer, however, to Nicolls' summons he submitted a long justification of the Dutch title; yet while protesting against any breach of the peace between the King and the States-General, "for the hinderance and prevention of all differences and the spilling of innocent blood, not only in these parts, but also in Europe," he offered to treat. "Long Island is gone and lost;" the capital "can not hold out long," was the last dispatch to the "Lord Majors" of New Netherlands, which its director sent off that night "in silence through Hell Gate."

Observing Stuyvesant's reluctance to surrender, Nicolls directed Captain Hyde, who commanded the squadron, to reduce the fort. Two of the ships accordingly landed their troops just below Breuckelen (Brooklyn), where volunteers from New England and the Long Island villages had already encamped. The other two, coming up with full sail, passed in front of Fort Amsterdam and anchored between it and Nutten Island.[2] Standing on one of the angles of the fortress—an artilleryman with a lighted match at his side—the director watched their approach. At this moment the two domines Megapolensis, imploring him not to begin hostilities, led Stuyvesant from the rampart, who then, with a hundred of the garrison, went into the city to resist the landing of the English. Hoping on against hope, the director now sent Counsellor de Decker, Secretary Van Ruypen, Burgomaster Steenwyck, and "Schepen" Cousseau with a letter to Nicolls stating that, as he felt bound "to stand the storm," he desired if possible to arrange on accommodation. But the English commander merely declared, "To-morrow I will speak with you at Manhattan."

"Friends," was the answer, "will be welcome if they come in a friendly manner."

"I shall come with ships and soldiers," replied Nicolls; "raise the white flag of peace at the fort, and then something may be considered."

When this imperious message became known, men, women, and children flocked to the director, beseeching him to submit. His only answer was, "I would rather be carried out dead." The next day the city authorities, the clergymen, and the officers of the burgher guard, assembling at the Stadt-Huys, at the suggestion of Domine Megapolensis, adopted a remonstrance to the director, exhibiting the hopeless situation of New Amsterdam, on all sides "encompassed and hemmed in by enemies," and protesting against any further opposition to

[2] Now called Governor's Island.

the will of God. Besides the *schout,* burgomasters, and schepens, the remonstrance was signed by Wilmerdonck and eighty-five of the principal inhabitants, among whom was Stuyvesant's own son, Balthazar.

At last the director was obliged to yield. Although there were now fifteen hundred souls in New Amsterdam, there were not more than two hundred and fifty men able to bear arms, besides the one hundred fifty regular soldiers. The people had at length refused to be called out, and the regular troops were already heard talking of "where booty is to be found, and where the young women live who wear gold chains." The city, entirely open along both rivers, was shut on the northern side by a breastwork and palisades[3], which, though sufficient to keep out the savages, afforded no defense against a military siege. There were scarcely six hundred pounds of serviceable powder in store.

A council of war had reported Fort Amsterdam untenable; for though it mounted twenty-four guns, its single wall of earth, not more than ten feet high and four thick, was almost touched by the private dwellings clustered around, and was commanded, within a pistol-shot, by hills on the north, over which ran the "Heereweg" or Broadway.

Upon the faith of Nicolls' promise to deliver back the city and fort "in case the difference of the limits of this province be agreed upon betwixt his majesty of England and the high and mighty States-General," Stuyvesant now commissioned

[3] A fortification from which has come the modern name of Wall Street.

Counsellor John de Decker, Captain Nicholas Varlett, Dr. Samuel Megapolensis, Burgomaster Cornelius Steenwyck, old Burgomaster Oloff Stevenson van Cortlandt, and old Schepen Jacques Cousseau to agree upon articles with the English commander or his representatives. Nicolls, on his part, appointed Sir Robert Carr and Colonel George Cartwright, John Winthrop, and Samuel Willys, of Connecticut, and Thomas Clarke and John Pynchon, of Massachusetts. "The reason why those of Boston and Connecticut were joined," afterward explained the royal commander, "was because those two colonies should hold themselves the more engaged with us if the Dutch had been overconfident of their strength."

At eight o'clock the next morning, which was Saturday, the commissioners on both sides met at Stuyvesant's "bouwery" and arranged the terms of capitulation. The only difference which arose was respecting the Dutch soldiers, whom the English refused to convey back to Holland. The articles of capitulation promised the Dutch security in their property, customs of inheritance, liberty of conscience and church discipline. The municipal officers of Manhattan were to continue for the present unchanged, and the town was to be allowed to chose deputies, with "free voices in all public affairs." Owners of property in Fort Orange might, if they pleased, "slight the fortifications there," and enjoy their houses "as people do where there is no fort."

For six months there was to be free intercourse with Holland. Public records were to be respected. The articles, consented to by Nicolls, were to be ratified by Stuyvesant the next Monday morning at eight o'clock, and within two hours afterward, the "fort and town called New Amsterdam, upon the Isle of Manhatoes," were to be delivered up, and the military officers and soldiers were to "march out with their arms, drums beating, and colors flying, and lighted matches."

On the following Monday morning at eight o'clock Stuyvesant, at the head of the garrison, marched out of Fort Amsterdam with all the honors of war, and led his soldiers down the Beaver Lane to the water-side, whence they were embarked for Holland. An English corporal's guard at the same time took possession of the fort; and Nicolls and Carr, with their two companies, about a hundred seventy strong, entered the city, while Cartwright took possession of the gates and the Stadt-Huys. The New England and Long Island volunteers, however, were prudently kept at the Breuckelen ferry, as the citizens dreaded most being plundered by them. The English flag was hoisted on Fort Amsterdam, the name of which was immediately changed to "Fort James." Nicolls was now proclaimed by the burgomasters deputy-governor for the Duke of York, in compliment to whom he directed that the city of New Amsterdam should thenceforth be known as "New York."

To Nicolls' European eye the Dutch metropolis, with its earthen fort, enclosing a windmill and high flag-staff, a prison and a governor's house, and a double-roofed church, above which loomed a square tower, its gallows and whipping-post at the river's side, and its rows of houses which hugged the citadel, presented but a mean appearance. Yet before long he described it to the Duke as "the best of all his majesty's towns in America," and assured his royal highness that, with proper management, "within five years the staple of America will be drawn hither, of which the brethren of Boston are very sensible." . . .

The reduction of New Netherlands was now accomplished. All that could be further done was to change its name; and, to glorify one of the most bigoted princes in English history, the royal province was ordered to be called "New York." Ignorant of James' grant of New Jersey to Berkeley and Carteret, Nicolls gave to the region west of the Hudson the name of "Albania," and to Long Island that of "Yorkshire," so as to comprehend all the titles of the Duke of York. The flag of England was at length triumphantly displayed, where, for half a century, that of Holland had rightfuly waved; and from Virginia to Canada, the King of Great Britain was acknowledged as sovereign.

Viewed in all its aspects, the event which gave to the whole of that country a unity in allegiance, and to which a misgoverned people complacently submitted, was as inevitable as it was momentous. But whatever may have been its ultimate consequences, this treacherous and violent seizure of the territory and possessions of an unsuspecting ally was no less a breach of private justice than of public faith.

It may, indeed, be affirmed that, among all the acts of selfish perfidy which royal ingratitude conceived and executed, there have been few more characteristic and none more base.

BACON'S REBELLION IN VIRGINIA

(1676)

BY AN ANONYMOUS WRITER[1]

There is no nation this day under the copes of
Heaven can so experimentaly speak the sad effects
of men of great parts being reduc't to necessity, as
England; but not to rake up the notorious misde-
meanours of the dead, I shall endeavour to prevent the sad effects of so deplorable a cause, by
giving you an account of the remarkable life
and death of this gentleman of whom I am about
to discourse. And because when a man has once
ingag'd himself in an ill action, all men are ready
to heap an innumerable aspersions upon him, of
which he is no ways guilty, I shall be so just in the
History of his Life as not to rob him of those
commendations which his Birth and Acquisitions
claim as due, and so kind both to Loyalty and the
wholsom constituted Laws of our Kingdom, as not

[1] This account was written a year after the events described by an author whose name is unknown. Internal
evidence points to his intimate personal knowledge of what
took place. Writing after the failure of the rebellion; moreover, after Bacon himself was dead, and the strong popular
movement led by him had consequently much disintegrated,
the writer's view is naturally somewhat out of sympathy with
Bacon. Printed in Hart's "American History Told by Contemporaries."

John Esten Cooke, in his "History of Virginia," declares
that Bacon was "the soul of the rebellion" and his rising
"not a hair-brained project, but the result of deliberate cal-
culation." As a representative of the Virginia people Bacon

to smother any thing which would render him to blame.

This Gentleman who has of late becconed the attention of all men of understanding who are any ways desirous of Novelty, [or] care what becomes of any part of the World besides that themselves live in, had the honour to be descended of an Ancient and Honourable Family, his name Nathanael Bacon, to whom to the long known Title of Gentleman, by his long study [at] the Inns of Court he has since added that of Esquire. He was the Son of Mr. Thomas Bacon of an ancient Seat known by the denomination of Freestone-Hall, in the County of Suffolk, a Gentleman of known loyalty and ability. His Father as he was able so he was willing to allow this his Son a very Gentile Competency to subsist upon, but he as it proved having a Soul too large for that allowance, could not contain himself within bounds; which his careful Father perceiving, and also that he had a mind to Travel (having seen divers parts of the World before) consented to his inclination of going to Virginia, and accommodated him with a Stock for that purpose, to the value of 1,800l. Starling, as I am credibly informed by a Merchant of very good wealth, who is now in this City, and had the fortune to carry him thither.

He began his Voyage thitherwards about Three

"protested strongly against public grievances, compelling redress." He anticipated that the country would profit from his uprising, "and his anticipation was justified." The result as against Berkeley, "compelled the dissolution of the Royal Assembly, which had remained unchanged since 1660, and resulted in 'Bacon's assembly,' which began by raising the public revenue, extending suffrage to freemen, and was so defiant that Berkeley dissolved it."

years since, and lived for about a years space in that Continent in very good repute, his extraordinary parts like a Letter of recommendation rendring him aceptable in all mens company, whilst his considerable Concerns in that place were able to bear him out in the best of Society. These Accomplishments of mind and fortune rendred him so remarkable, that the worthy Governour of that Continent thought it requisite to take him into his Privy Council.

That Plantation which he chose to settle in is generally known by the name of Curles, situate in the upper part of James River and the time of his revolt was not till the beginning of March, 1675-6. At which time the Susquo-hannan Indians (a known Enemy to that Country) having made an Insurrection, and kild divers of the English, amongst whom it was his misfortune to have a Servant slain; in revenge of whose death, and other dammage(s) he received from those turbulent Susquo-hanians, without the Governeur's consent he furiously took up Arms against them, and was so fortunate as to put them to flight, but not content therewith; the aforesaid Governour hearing of his eager pursuit after the vanquisht Indians, sent out a select Company of Souldiers to command him to desist; but he instead of listning thereunto, persisted in his Revenge, and sent to the Governour to intreat his Commission, that he might more chearfully prosecute his design; which being denyed him by the Messenger he sent for that purpose, he notwithstanding continued to make head with his own Servants, and other English then resident in Curles against them.

In this interim the people of Henrica had returned him Burgess of their county; and he in order thereunto took his own Sloop and came down towards James Town, conducted by thirty odd Souldiers, with part of which he came ashore to Mr. Laurences House, to understand whether he might come in with safety or not, but being discovered by one Parson Clough, and also it being perceived that he had lined the Bushes of the said Town with Souldiers, the Governour thereupon ordered an allarm to be beaten through the whole Town, which took so hot, that Bacon thinking himself not secure whilst he remained there within reach of their Fort, immediately commanded his men aboard, and tow'd his Sloop up the River; which the Governour perceiving, ordered the Ships which lay at Sandy-point to pursue and take him; and they by the industry of their Commanders succeeded so well in the attempt, that they presently stopt his passage; so that Mr. Bacon finding himself pursued both before and behind, after some capitulations, quietly surrendered himself Prisoner to the Governours Commissioners, to the great satisfaction of all his Friends; which action of his was so obliging to the Governour, that he granted him his liberty immediately upon Paroll, without confining him either to Prison or Chamber, and the next day, after some private discourse passed betwixt the Governour, the Privy Council, and himself, he was amply restored to all his former Honours and Dignities, and a Commission partly promised him to be General against the Indian Army; but upon further enquiry into his Affairs it was not thought fit to be granted him; whereat his ambitious mind seem'd mightily to be displeas'd; insomuch that he gave out, that it was his intention to sell his whole concerns in Virginia, and to go with his whole Family to live either in Merry-land or the South, because he would avoid (as he said) the scandal of being accounted a factious person there.

But this resolution it seems was but a pretence, for afterwards he headed the same Runnagado English that he formerly found ready to undertake and go sharers with him in any of his Rebellions, and adding to them the assistance of his own Slaves and Servants, headed them so far till they toucht at the Occonegies Town, where he was treated very civilly, and by the Inhabitants informed where some of the Susquohanno's were inforted, whom presently he assails, and after he had vanquished them, slew about seventy of them in their Fort: But as he returned back to the Occoneges, he found they had fortified themselves with divers more Indians than they had at his first arrival; wherefore he desired Hostages of them for their good behaviour, whilst he and his followers lay within command of their Fort. But those treacherous Indians grown confident by reason of their late recruit, returned him this Answer, That their Guns were the only Hostages he was like to have of them, and if he would have them he must fetch them. Which was no soner spoke, but the Indians salied out of the Fort and shot one of his Sentinels, whereupon he charged them so fiercely, that the Fight continued not only all that day, but the next also, till the approach of the Evening, at which time finding his men grow faint for want of Provision, he laid hold of the opportunity, being befriended by a gloomy night, and so made an honourable retreat homewards.

Howbeit we may judge what respect he had gain'd in James-Town by this subsequent transaction.

When he was first brought hither it was frequently reported among the Commonalty that he was kept close Prisoner, which report caused the people of that Town, those of Charles-city, Henrico, and New-Kent Countries, being in all about the Number of eight hundred, or a thousand, to rise and march thitherwards in order to his rescue; whereupon the Governor was forced to desire Mr. Bacon to go himself in Person, and by his open appearance quiet the people.

This being past, Mr. Bacon, about the 25th of June last, dissatisfied that he could not have a Commission granted him to go against the Indians, in the night time departed the Town unknown to any body, and about a week after got together between four and five hundred men of New-Kent County, with whom he marched to James-Town, and drew up in order before the House of State; and there peremptorily demanded of the Governor, Council and Burgesses (there then collected) a Commission to go against the Indians, which if they should refuse to grant him, he told them that neither he nor ne're a man in his Company would depart from their Doors till he had obtained his request; whereupon to prevent farther danger in so great an exigence, the Council and Burgesses by much intreaty obtain'd him a Commission Signed by the Governor, an Act for one thousand men to be Listed under his command to go against the Indians, to whom the same pay was to be granted as was allowed to them who went against the Fort. But Bacon was not satisfied with this, but afterwards earnestly importuned,

and at length obtained of the House, to pass an
Act of Indemnity to all Persons who had sided
with him, and also Letters of recommendations
from the Governor to his Majesty in his behalf;
and moreover caused Collonel Claybourn and his
Son, Captain Claybourn, Lieutenant Collonel West,
and Lieutenant Collonel Hill, and many others, to
be degraded for ever bearing any Office, whether
it were Military or Civil.

Having obtained these large Civilities of the
Governor, &c. one would have thought that if the
Principles of honesty would not have obliged him
to peace and loyalty, those of gratitude should.
But, alas, when men have been once flusht or entred
with Vice, how hard is it for them to leave it, especially it tends towards ambition or greatness, which
is the general lust of a large Soul, and the common error of vast parts, which fix their Eyes so
upon the lure of greatness, that they have no time
left them to consider by what indirect and unlaw-
ful means they must (if ever) attain it.

This certainly was Mr. Bacon's Crime, who, after
he had once lanched into Rebellion, nay, and upon
submission had been pardoned for it, and also
restored, as if he had committed no such hainous
offence, to his former honour and dignities (which
weer considerable enough to content any reasonable mind) yet for all this he could not forbear
wading into his former misdemeanors, and continued his opposition against that prudent and established Government, ordered by his Majesty of
Great Brittain to be duely observed in that Continent.

In fine, he continued (I cannot say properly in
the Fields, but) in the Woods with a considerable

Army all last Summer, and maintain'd several Brushes with the Governors Party: sometime routing them, and burning all before him, to the great damage of many of his Majesties loyal Subjects there resident; sometimes he and his Rebels were beaten by the Governor, &c., and forc't to run for shelter amongst the Woods and Swomps. In which lamentable condition that unhappy Continent has remain'd for the space of almost a Twelve-month, every one therein that were able being forc't to take up Arms for security of their own lives, and no one reckoning their Goods, Wives, or Children to be their own, since they were so dangerously expos'd to the doubtful Accidents of an uncertain War.

But the indulgent Heavens, who are alone able to compute what measure of punishments are adequate or fit for the sins of transgressions of a Nation, has in its great mercy thought fit to put a stop, at least, if not a total period and conclusion to these Virginian troubles, by the death of this Nat. Bacon, the great Molestor of the quiet of that miserable Nation; so that now we who are here in England, and have any Relations or Correspondence with any of the Inhabitants of that Continent, may by the arrival of the next Ships from that Coast expect to hear that they are freed from all their dangers, quitted of all their fears, and in great hopes and expectations to live quietly under their own Vines, and enjoy the benefit of their commendable labours.

I know it is by some reported that this Mr. Bacon was a very hard drinker, and that he dyed by inbibing, or taking in two much Brandy. But I am informed by those who are Persons of undoubted Reputation, and had the happiness to see the same Letter which gave his Majesty an account of his death, that there was no such thing therein mentioned: he was certainly a Person indued with great natural parts, which notwithstanding his juvenile extravagances he had adorned with many elaborate acquisitions, and by the help of learning and study knew how to manage them to a Miracle, it being the general vogue of all that knew him, that he usually spoke as much sense in as few words, and delivered that sense as opportunely as any they ever kept company withal: Wherefore as I am my self a Lover of Ingenuity, though an abhorrer of disturbance or Rebellion, I think fit since Providence was pleased to let him dye a Natural death in his Bed, not to asperse him with saying he kill'd himself with drinking.

KING PHILIP'S WAR

(1676)

BY WILLIAM HUBBARD [1]

The Occasion of Philips so sudden taking up
Arms the last Year, was this: There was one
John Sausaman, a very cunning and plausible Indian, well skilled in the English Language, and
bred up in the Profession of Christian Religion,
employed as a Schoolmaster at Natick, the Indian
Town, who upon some Misdemeanor fled from his
Place to Philip, by whom he was entertained in
the Room and Office of Secretary, and his chief
Councellor, whom he trusted with all his Affairs
and secret Counsels: But afterwards, whether upon
the Sting of his own Conscience, or by the frequent Sollicitations of Mr. Eliot, that had known
him from a Child, and instructed him in the Principles of our Religion, who was often laying before him the heinous Sin of his Apostasy, and returning back to his old Vomit; he was at last
prevailed with to forsake Philip, and return back
to the Christian Indians at Natick where he was
baptised, manifested publick Repentance for all

[1] From Hubbard's "Narrative of the Troubles with the
Indians of New England." Hubbard was graduated from
Harvard in 1642 in the first class sent out by the college.
In 1666 he was settled as minister at Ipswich, Mass., and
died in 1704. His qualities as a minister, his learning and
his ability as a writer were praised by John Eliot, the apostle
to the Indians.

his former Offences, [15] and made a serious profession of the Christian Religion; and did apply himself to preach to the Indians, wherein he was better gifted than any other of the Indian Nation; so as he was observed to conform more to the English Manners than any other Indian.

Yet having Occasion to go up with some others of his Country men to Namasket, whether for the Advantage of Fishing or some such Occasion, it matters not; being there not far from Phillips Country, he had Occasion to be much in the Company of Philips Indians, and of Philip himself: by which Means he discerned by several Circumstances that the Indians were plotting anew against us; the which out of Faithfulness to the English the said Sausaman informed the Governour of; adding also, that if it were known that he revealed it, he knew they would presently kill him. There appearing so many concurrent Testimonies from others, making it the more probable, that there was certain Truth in the Information; some Inquiry was made into the Business, by examining Philip himself, several of his Indians, who although they could do nothing, yet could not free themselves from just Suspicion; Philip therefore soon after contrived the said Sausamans Death, which was strangely discovered; notwithstanding it was so cunningly effected, for they that murdered him, met him upon the Ice on a great Pond, and presently after they had knocked him down, put him under the Ice, yet leaving his Gun and his Hat upon the Ice, that it might be thought he fell in accidentally through the Ice and was drowned: but being missed by his Friend, who finding his Hat and his Gun, they were thereby

led to the Place, where his Body was found under
the Ice: when they took it up to bury him, some of
his Friends, specially one David, observed some
Bruises about his Head, which made them suspect
he was first knocked down, before he was put into
the Water: however, they buried him near about
the Place where he was found, without making
any further Inquiry at present: nevertheless David
his Friend, reported these Things to some English at Taunton (a Town not far from Namasket),
occasioned the Governour to inquire further into
the Business, wisely considering, that as Sausaman had told him, If it were known that he had
revealed any of their Plots, they would murder
him for his Pains.

Wherefore by special Warrant the Body of
Sausaman being digged again out of his Grave,
it was very apparent that he had been killed, and
not drowned. And by a strange Providence an
Indian was found, that by Accident was standing
unseen upon a Hill, had seen them murther the
said Sausaman, but durst never reveal it for Fear
of losing his own Life likewise, until he was
called to the Court at Plimouth, or before the Governour, where he plainly [16] confessed what he
had seen. The Murderers being apprehended,
were convicted by his undeniable Testimony, and
other remarkable Circumstances, and so were all
put to Death, being but three in Number; the last
of them confessed immediately before his Death,
that his Father (one of the Councellors and
special Friends of Philip) was one of the two that
murdered Sausaman, himself only looking on.

This was done at Plimouth Court, held in June,
1674. Insomuch that Philip apprehending the

Danger his own Head was in next, never used any further Means to clear himself from what was like to be laid to his Charge, either about his plotting against the English, nor yet about Sausamans Death: but by keeping his Men continually about him in Arms, and gathering what Strangers he could to join with him, marching up and down constantly in Arms, both all the while the Court sat, as well as afterwards. The English of Plimouth hearing of all this, yet took no further Notice, than only to order a Militia Watch in all the adjacent Towns, hoping that Philip finding himself not likely to be arraigned by Order of the said Court, the present Cloud might blow over, as some others of like Nature had done before; but in Conclusion, the Matter proved otherwise; for Philip finding his Strength daily increasing, by the flocking of Neighbour-Indians unto him, and sending over their Wives and Children to the Narhagansets for Security (as they use to do when they intend War with any of their Enemies,) immediately they began to alarm the English at Swanzy, (the next Town to Philips Country,) as it were daring the English to begin; at last their Insolencies grew to such an Height, that they began not only to use threatening Words to the English, but also to kill their Cattel and rifle their Houses; whereat an English-man was so provoked, that he let fly a Gun at an Indian, but did only wound, not kill him; whereupon the Indians immediately began to kill all the English they could, so as on the 24th of June, 1675, was the Alarm of War first sounded in Plimouth Colony, when eight or nine of the English were slain in and about Swanzy. . . .

About this Time several Parties of English, within Plimouth Jurisdiction, were willing to have a Hand in so good a Matter, as catching of Philip would be, who perceiving that he was now going down the Wind, were willing to hasten his Fall. Amongst others, a small Party, July 31 [1676], went out of Bridgewater upon discovery, and by Providence were directed to fall upon a Company of Indians where Philip was; they came up with them, and killed some of his special Friends; Philip himself was next to his Uncle, that was shot down, and had the Soldier had his Choice which to shoot at, known which had been the right Bird, he might as well have taken him as his Uncle, but 'tis said that he had newly cut off his Hair, that he might not be known: the Party that did this Exploit were few in Number, and therefore not being able to keep altogether close in the Reer, that cunning Fox escaped away through the Bushes undiscerned, in the Reer of the English. . . .

Within two Days after, Capt Church, the Terror of the Indians in Plimouth Colony, marching in pursuit of Philip, with but thirty English-men, and twenty reconciled Indians, took twenty three of the Enemy, and the next Day following them by their Tracts, fell upon their Head-Quarters, and killed and took about an hundred and thirty of them, but with the Loss of one English Man; in this Engagement God did appear in a more than ordinary Manner to fight for the English: for the Indians by their Number, and other Advantages of the Place, were so conveniently provided, that they might have made the first Shot at the English, and done them much Damage; but one of their own Country-men in Capt. Church's Company espying them, called aloud unto them in their own Language, telling them that if they shot a Gun, they were all dead Men; with which they were so amazed, that they durst not once offer to fire at the English, which made the Victory the more remarkable: Philip made a very narrow Escape at that Time, being forced to leave his Treasures, his beloved Wife and only Son to the Mercy of the English, Skin for Skin, all that a Man hath will he give for his Life.

His Ruine being thus gradually carried on, his Misery was not prevented but augmented thereby; being himself made acquainted with the Sence and experimental Feeling of the captivity of his Children, loss of his Friends, slaughter of his Subjects, bereavement of all Family Relations, and being stript of all outward Comforts, before his own Life should be taken away. Such Sentence sometimes passed upon Cain, made him cry out, that his Punishment was greater than he could bear.

This bloody Wretch had one Week or two more to live, an Object of Pity, but a Spectacle of Divine Vengeance; his own Followers beginning now to plot against his Life, to make the better Terms for their own, as they did also seek to betray Squaw Sachim of Pocasset, Philips near Kinswoman and Confederate. . . .

Philip, like a Salvage and wild Beast, having been hunted by the English Forces through the Woods, above an hundred Miles backward and forward, at last was driven to his own Den, upon Mount-hope, where retiring himself with a few of his best Friends into a Swamp, which proved but a Prison to keep him safe, till the Messengers

of Death came by Divine Permission to execute
Vengeance upon him, which was thus accomplished.

Such had been his inveterate Malice and Wickedness against the English, that despairing of
Mercy from them, he could not bear that any thing
should be suggested to him about a Peace, insomuch as he caused one of his Confederates to be
killed for propounding an Expedient of Peace;
which so provoked some of his Company, not altogether so desperate as himself, that one of them
(being near of kin that was killed) fled to Road-Island (whither, that active Champion Capt.
Church was newly retired, to recruit his Men for
a little Time, being much tired with hard Marches
all that Week) informing them that Philip was
fled to a Swamp in Mount-hope whither he would
undertake to lead them that would pursue him.
This was welcome News, and the best Cordial for
such martial Spirits: whereupon he immediately
with a small Company of Men, part English and
part Indians, began another March, which shall
prove fatal to Philip, and end that Controversie
betwixt the English and him: for coming very
early to the side of the Swamp, his Soldiers began
presently to surround it, and whether the Devil appeared to him in a Dream that Night, as he did
unto Saul, forboding his tragical End (it matters
not); as he intended to make his Escape out of
the Swamp, he was shot through the Heart by an
Indian of his own Nation, as is said, that had all
this while kept himself in a Neutrality until this
Time, but now had the casting-vote in his Power,
by which he determined the Quarrel that had held
so long in Suspense.

179

THE FOUNDING OF PENNSYLVANIA

I

PENN'S ACCOUNT OF THE COLONY[1]

(1684)

The first planters in these parts were the Dutch,
and soon after them the Swedes and Finns. The
Dutch applied themselves to traffic, the Swedes
and Finns to husbandry. There were some disputes between them for some years; the Dutch
looking upon them as intruders upon their purchase and possession, which was finally ended in the
surrender made by John Rizeing, the Swedish governor, to Peter Stuyvesant, governor for the
States of Holland, anno 1655.

The Dutch inhabit mostly those parts of the
province that lie upon or near the bay, and the
Swedes the freshes of the river Delaware. There
is no need of giving any description of them, who
are better known there than here; but they are a
plain, strong, industrious people, yet have made
no great progress in culture, or propagation of
fruit-trees; as if they desired rather to have enough

[1] Penn had already been part proprietor of West Jersey
when in 1681 he received the grant of Pennsylvania, as
compensation for a claim of his father's estate against the
English Government. He came out in person to America in
1682, made his famous treaty with the Indians and founded
Philadelphia. He returned to England in 1684, and again
visited Pennsylvania in 1699-1701. His account is printed
in Hart's "American History Told by Contemporaries."

than plenty or traffic. But I presume the Indians made them the more careless by furnishing them with the means of profit, to wit, skins and furs for rum and such strong liquors. They kindly received me as well as the English, who were few before the people concerned with me came among them. I must needs commend their respect to authority, and kind behaviour to the English. They do not degenerate from the old friendship between both kingdoms. As they are people proper and strong of body, so they have fine children, and almost every house full: rare to find one of them without three or four boys and as many girls; some six, seven, and eight sons. And I must do them that right, I see few young men more sober and laborious.

The Dutch have a meeting-place for religious worship at Newcastle; and the Swedes three; one at Christina, one at Tenecum, and one at Wicoco, within half a mile of this town.

There rests that I speak of the condition we are in, and what settlement we have made; in which I will be as short as I can. The country lieth bounded on the east by the river and bay of Delaware and Eastern Sea. It hath the advantage of many creeks, or rivers, that run into the main river or bay, some navigable for great ships, some for small craft. Those of most eminency are Christina, Brandywine, Skilpot, and Sculkil, any one of which has room to lay up the royal navy of England, there being from four to eight fathom of water.

The lesser creeks or rivers, yet convenient for sloops and ketches of good burthen, are Lewis, Mespillion, Cedar, Dover, Cranbrook, Feversham, and Georges below; and Chichester, Chester, Toacawny, Pammapecka, Portquessin, Neshimenck, and Pennberry in the freshes: many lesser, that admit boats and shallops. Our people are mostly settled upon the upper rivers, which are pleasant and sweet, and generally bounded with good land.

The planted part of the province and territories is cast into six counties: Philadelphia, Buckingham, Chester, Newcastle, Kent, and Sussex, containing about four thousand souls. Two general assemblies have been held, and with such concord and despatch that they sat but three weeks, and at least seventy laws were passed without one dissent in any material thing. But of this more hereafter, being yet raw and new in our gear. However, I cannot forget their singular respect to me in this infancy of things, who, by their own private expenses, so early considered mine for the public, as to present me with an impost upon certain goods imported and exported, which, after my acknowledgment of their affection, I did as freely remit to the province and the traders to it. And for the well-government of the said counties, courts of justice are established in every county, with proper officers, as justices, sheriffs, clerks, constables; which courts are held every two months. But, to prevent lawsuits, there are three peacemakers chosen by every county court, in the nature of common arbitrators, to hear and end differences between man and man. And spring and fall there is an orphans' court in each county, to inspect and regulate the affairs of orphans and widows.

Philadelphia: the expectation of those who are concerned in this province is at last laid out, to the great content of those here who are any ways

interested therein. The situation is a neck of
land, and lieth between two navigable rivers, Delaware and Sculkill, whereby it hath two fronts upon
the water, each a mile, and two from river to
river. Delaware is a glorious river; but the Sculkill, being an hundred miles boatable above the
falls, and its course north-east toward the foun-
tain of Susquehannah, (that tends to the heart of
the province, and both sides our own), it is like
to be a great part of the settlement of this age. I
say little of the town itself, because a platform
will be shown you by my agent, in which those
who are purchasers of me, will find their names
and interests. But this I will say, for the good
providence of God, that of all the many places I
have seen in the world, I remember not one better
seated; so that it seems to me to have been appointed for a town, whether we regard the rivers,
or the conveniency of the coves, ducks, and springs,
the loftiness and soundness of the land, and the
air, held by the people of those parts to be very
good.

It is advanced within less than a year, to
about fourscore houses and cottages, such as they
are, where merchants and handicrafts are following their vocations as fast as they can; while the
countrymen are close at their farms. Some of
them got a little winter corn in the ground last
season; and the generality have had a handsome
summer-crop, and are preparing for their winter
corn. They reaped their barley this year, in the
month called May, the wheat in the month following; so that there is time in these parts for another crop of divers things before the winter season. We are daily in hopes of shipping to add to

our number; for, blessed be God! here is both room and accommodation for them: the stories of our necessity being either the fear of our friends, or the scarecrows of our enemies; for the greatest hardship we have suffered hath been salt meat, which, by fowl in winter and fish in summer, together with some poultry, lamb, mutton, veal, and plenty of venison, the best part of the year, hath been made very passable. I bless God I am fully satisfied with the country and entertainment I got in it; for I find that particular content, which hath always attended me, where God in his providence hath made it my place and service to reside. You cannot imagine my station can be at present free of more than ordinary business; and, as such, I may say it is a troublesome work. But the method things are putting in will facilitate the charge, and give an easier motion to the administration of affairs. However, as it is some men's duty to plow, some to sow, some to water, and some to reap, so it is the wisdom as well as the duty of a man to yield to the mind of providence, and cheerfully as well as carefully embrace and follow the guidance of it.

II

PENN'S TREATY WITH THE INDIANS

(1683)

HIS OWN ACCOUNT

Every king hath his council; and that consists of all the old and wise men of his nation, which perhaps is two hundred people. Nothing of moment is undertaken, be it war, peace, selling of land, or traffic, without advising with them, and, which is more, with the young men, too. It is admirable to consider how powerful the kings are, and yet how they move by the breath of their people. I have had occasion to be in council with them upon treaties for land, and to adjust the terms of trade.

Their order is thus: The king sits in the middle of an half-moon, and has his council, the old and wise, on each hand. Behind them, or at a little distance, sit the younger fry in the same figure. Having consulted and resolved their business, the king ordered one of them to speak to me. He stood up, came to me, and in the name of the king saluted me, then took me by the hand, and told me that he was ordered by his king to speak to me, and that now it was not he but the king who spoke, because what he should say was the king's mind. He first prayed

---

[1] Letter from Penn to the Free Society of Traders, dated Aug. 16, 1683.

me to excuse them, that they had not complied
with me the last time. He feared there might be
some fault in the interpreter, being neither Indian nor English. Besides, it was the Indian cus-
tom to deliberate and take up much time in council before they resolved; and that, if the young
people and owners of the land had been as ready
as he, I had not met with so much delay.

Having thus introduced his matter, he fell to
the bounds of the land they had agreed to dispose
of, and the price; which now is little and dear,
that which would have bought twenty miles not
buying now two. During the time that this person
spoke, not a man of them was observed to whis-
per or smile—the old grave, the young reverent,
in their deportment. They speak little, but fer-
vently, and with elegance. I have never seen more
natural sagacity, considering them without the
help (I was going to say the spoil) of tradition:
and he will deserve the name of wise who outwits
them in any treaty about a thing they understand.

When the purchase was agreed, great promises
passed between us of kindness and good neighborhood, and that the English and Indians must
live in love as long as the sun gave light; which
done, another made a speech to the Indians, in
the name of all the sachamakers or kings; first, to
tell them what was done; next, to charge and command them to love the Christians, and particularly
to live in peace with me and the people under my
goverment; that many governors had been in
the river; but that no governor had come himself
to live and stay here before; and having now such
an one, who had treated them well, they should
never do him or his any wrong; at every sentence

of which they shouted, and said Amen in their way. . . .

We have agreed, that in all differences between us, six of each side shall end the matter. Do not abuse them, but let them have justice, and you win them.

III

THE REALITY OF PENN'S TREATY

(1682)

BY GEORGE E. ELLIS [1]

There has been much discussion of late years concerning the far-famed Treaty of Penn with the Indians. A circumstance, which has all the interest both of fact and of poetry, was confirmed by such unbroken testimony of tradition that history seemed to have innumerable records of it in the hearts and memories of each generation. But as there appears no document or parchment of such *criteria* as to satisfy all inquiries, historical skepticism has ventured upon the absurd length of calling in question the fact of the treaty. The Historical Society of Pennsylvania, with commendable zeal, has bestowed much labor upon the questions connected with the treaty, and the results which have been attained can scarcely fail to satisfy a candid inquirer. All claim to a peculiar distinction for William Penn, on account of the

[1] Mr. Ellis was a Unitarian clergyman, long pastor of a church at Charlestown, Mass.

singularity of his just proceedings in this matter is candidly waived, because the Swedes, the Dutch, and the English had previously dealt thus justly with the natives. It is in comparison with Pizarro and Cortés that the colonists of all other nations in America appear to an advantage; but the fame of William Penn stands, and ever will stand, preeminent for unexceptionable justice and peace in his relations with the natives.

Penn had several meetings for conference and treaties with the Indians, besides those which he held for the purchase of lands. But unbroken and reverently cherished tradition, beyond all possibility of contradiction, has designated one great treaty held under a large elm-tree, at Shackamaxon (now Kensington)², a treaty which Voltaire justly characterizes as "never sworn to, and never broken." In Penn's Letter to the Free Society of Traders, dated August 16, 1683, he refers to his conferences with the Indians. Two deeds, conveying land to him, are on record, both of which bear an earlier date than this letter; namely, June 23d and July 14th of the same year. He had designed to make a purchase in May; but having been called off to a conference with Lord Baltimore, he postponed the business till June.

The "Great Treaty" was doubtless unconnected with the purchase of land, and was simply a treaty of amity and friendship, in confirmation of one previously held, by Penn's direction, by Markham, on the same spot; that being a place which the In-

² Kensington is now a part of Philadelphia, being the northeastern section. It lies on the Delaware River, about two miles distant from the City Hall, and is a center of the ship-building industry.

dians were wont to use for this purpose. It is probable that the treaty was held on the last of November, 1682; that the Delawares, the Mingos, and other Susquehanna tribes formed a large assembly on the occasion; that written minutes of the conference were made, and were in possession of Governor Gordon, who states nine conditions as belonging to them in 1728, but are now lost; and that the substance of the treaty is given in Penn's Letter to the Free Traders. These results are satisfactory, and are sufficient corroborated by known facts and documents. The Great Treaty, being distinct from a land purchase, is significantly distinguished in history and tradition.

The inventions of romance and imagination could scarcely gather round this engaging incident attractions surpassing in its own simple and impressive interest. Doubtless Clarkson has given a fair representation of it, if we merely disconnect from his account the statement that the Indians were armed, and all that confounds the treaty of friendship with the purchase of lands. Penn wore a sky-blue sash of silk around his waist, as the most simple badge. The pledges there given were to hold their sanctity "while the creeks and rivers run, and while the sun, moon, and stars endure."

While the whites preserved in written records the memory of such covenants, the Indians had their methods for perpetuating in safe channels their own relations. They cherished in grateful regard, they repeated to their children and to the whites, the terms of the Great Treaty. The Delawares called William Penn *Miquon,* in their own language, though they seem to have adopted the name given him by the Iroquois, *Onas;* both which terms signify a quill or pen. Benjamin West's picture of the treaty is too imaginative for a historical piece. He makes Penn of a figure and aspect which would become twice the years that had passed over his head. The elm-tree was spared in the war of the American Revolution, when there was distress for firewood, the British officer, Simcoe, having placed a sentinel beneath it for protection. It was prostrated by the wind on the night of Saturday, March 3, 1810. It was of gigantic size, and the circles around its heart indicated an age of nearly three centuries. A piece of it was sent to the Penn mansion at Stoke Poges, in England, where it is properly commemorated. A marble monument, with suitable inscription was "placed by the Penn Society A. D. 1827 to mark the site of the Great Elm Tree."

THE CHARTER OAK AFFAIR IN CONNECTICUT

(1682)

BY ALEXANDER JOHNSTON[1]

In December, 1686, the Hartford authorities were called upon to measure their strength again with their old antagonist. Andros had landed at Boston, commissioned as governor of all New England, and bent on abrogating the charters. Following Dudley's lead, he wrote to Treat, suggesting that by this time the trial of the writs had certainly gone against the colony; and that the authorities would do much to commend the colony to his majesty's good pleasure by entering a formal surrender of the charter. The colony authorities were possibly as well versed in the law of the case as Andros, and they took good care to do nothing of the sort; and, as the event showed, they thus saved the charter.

The assembly met as usual in October, 1687; but their records show that they were in profound doubt and distress. Andros was with them, accompanied by some sixty regular soldiers, to enforce his demand for the charter. It is certain that he did not get it, tho the records, as usual, are cautious enough to give no reason why. Tradition

[1] From Johnston's "History of Connecticut." By permission of, and by arrangement with, the authorized publishers, Houghton, Mifflin Co. Copyright, 1887, by Alexander Johnston.

is responsible for the story of the charter oak. The assembly had met the royal governor in the meeting-house; the demand for the charter had been made; and the assembly had exhausted the resources of language to show to Andros how dear it was to them, and how impossible it was to give it up. Andros was immovable; he had watched that charter with longing eyes from the banks of the Hudson, and he had no intention of giving up his object now that the king had put him in power on the banks of the Connecticut.

Toward evening the case had become desperate. The little democracy was at last driven into a corner, where its old policy seemed no longer available; it must resist openly, or make a formal surrender of its charter. Just as the lights were lighted, the legal authorities yielded so far as to order the precious document to be brought in and laid on the table before the eyes of Andros. Then came a little more debate. Suddenly the lights were blown out; Captain Wadsworth, of Hartford, carried off the charter, and hid it in a hollow oak-tree on the estate of the Wyllyses, just across the "riveret;" and when the lights were relighted the colony was no longer able to comply with Andros's demand for a surrender.

Altho the account of the affair is traditional, it is difficult to see any good grounds for impeaching it on that account. It supplies, in the simplest and most natural manner, a blank in the Hartford proceedings of Andros which would otherwise be quite unaccountable. His plain purpose was to force Connecticut into a position where she must either surrender the charter or resist openly. He failed: the charter never was in his possession;

and the official records assign no reason for his failure. The colony was too prudent, and Andros too proud to put the true reason on record. Tradition supplies the gap with an exactness which proves itself.

Having done all that men could do, Treat and his associates bowed for the time to superior force. Andros was allowed to read his commission, and Treat, Fitz-John and Wait Winthrop, and John Allyn received appointments as members of his council for New England. John Allyn made what the governor doubtless considered to be the closing record for all time. But it is noteworthy that the record was so written as to flatter Andros's vanity, while it really put in terms a declaration of overpowering force, on which the commonwealth finally succeeded in saving her charter from invalidation. It is as follows:

"At a General Court at Hartford, October 31st, 1687, his excellency, Sir Edmund Andross, knight and Captain General and Governor of His Majesty's territories and dominions in New England, by order of His Majesty James the Second, King of England, Scotland, France, and Ireland, the 31st of October, 1687, took into his hands the government of the colony of Connecticut, it being by His Majesty annexed to Massachusetts and other colonies under his excellency's government.

"FINIS."

The government was destined to last far longer than either the governor or his government. But, while it lasted, Andros's government was bitterly hated, and with good reason. The reasons are more peculiarly appropriate to the history of Massachusetts, where they were felt more keenly than in Connecticut; but even in Connecticut, poor as was the field for plunder, and distant as it was from the "ring" which surrounded Andros, the exactions of the new system were wellnigh intolerable to a people whose annual expense of government had been carefully kept down to the lowest limits, so that, says Bancroft, they "did not exceed four thousand dollars; and the wages of the chief justice were ten shillings a day while on service." . . .

April, 1689, came at last. The people of Boston, at the first news of the English Revolution, clapped Andros into custody. May 9, the old Connecticut authorities quietly resumed their functions, and called the assembly together for the following month. William and Mary were proclaimed with great favor. Not a word was said about the disappearance or reapeparance of the charter; but the charter government was put into full effect again, as if Andros had never interrupted it. An address was sent to the king, asking that the charter be no further interfered with; but operations under it went on as before. No decided action was taken by the home government for some years, except that its appointment of the New York governor, Fletcher, to the command of the Connecticut militia, implied a decision that the Connecticut charter had been superseded.

Late in 1693 Fitz-John Winthrop was sent to England as agent to obtain a confirmation of the charter. He secured an emphatic legal opinion from Attorney General Somers, backed by those of Treby and Ward, that the charter was entirely valid, Treby's concurrent opinion taking this shape: "I am of the same opinion, and, as this matter is stated, there is no ground of doubt." The basis of the opinion was that the charter had been granted under the great seal; that it had not been surrendered under the common seal of the colony, nor had any judgment of record been entered against it; that its operation had merely been interfered with by overpowering force; that the charter therefore remained valid; and that the peaceable submission of the colony to Andros was merely an illegal suspension of lawful authority. In other words, the passive attitude of the colonial government had disarmed Andros so far as to stop the legal proceedings necessary to forfeit the charter; and then prompt action, at the critical moment, secured all that could be secured under the circumstances. William was willing enough to retain all possible fruits of James's tyranny, as he showed by enforcing the forfeiture of the Massachusetts charter; but the law in this case was too plain, and he ratified the lawyers' opinion in April, 1694. The charter had escaped its enemies at last, and its escape is a monument of one of the advantages of a real democracy.

THE COLONIZATION OF LOUISIANA

(1699)

BY CHARLES E. T. GAYARRÉ[1]

On February 27, 1699, Iberville and Bienville reached the Mississippi. When they approached its mouth they were struck with the gloomy magnificence of the sight. As far as the eye could reach, nothing was to be seen but reeds which rose five or six feet above the waters in which they bathed their roots. They waved mournfully under the blast of the sharp wind of the north, shivering in its icy grasp, as it tumbled, rolled, and gambolled on the pliant surface. Multitudes of birds of strange appearance, with their elongated shapes so lean that they looked like metamorphosed ghosts, clothed in plumage, screamed in the air, as if they were scared of one another. There was

[1] From Gayarré's "History of Louisiana" (1847). La Salle's expedition to the mouth of the Mississippi, when he took possession of the country in the name of the King of France, had taken place in 1682. Louis XIV in 1689 sent out an expedition to colonize the lower Mississippi. It comprized about two hundred men and was commanded by Sieur d'Iberville. Among his companions were two brothers, one of whom, Sieur de Bienville, was the real founder of New Orleans, and long served as Governor of Louisiana. Gayarré describes the arrival and experiences of these brothers.

Gayarré lived in New Orleans. He began to practise law there in 1830, and afterward served as reporter of the State Supreme Court. He died in 1895.

something agonizing in their shrieks that was in harmony with the desolation of the place. On every side of the vessel, monsters of the deep and huge alligators heaved themselves up heavily from their native or favorite element, and, floating lazily on the turbid waters, seemed to gaze at the intruders. . . .

It was a relief for the adventurers when, after having toiled up the river for ten days, they at last arrived at the village of the Bayagoulas. There they found a letter of Tonty to La Salle, dated in 1685. The letter, or rather that "speaking bark" as the Indians called it, had been preserved with great reverence. Tonty, having been informed that La Salle was coming with a fleet from France to settle a colony on the banks of the Mississippi, had not hesitated to set off from the northern lakes, with twenty Canadians and thirty Indians, and to come down to the Balize to meet his friend, who had failed to make out the mouth of the Mississippi, and had been landed by Beaujeu on the shores of Texas. After having waited for some time, and ignorant of what had happened, Tonty, with the same indifference to fatigues and dangers of an appalling nature, retraced his way back, leaving a letter to La Salle to inform him of his disappointment. Is there not something extremely romantic in the characters of the men of that epoch? Here is Tonty undertaking, with the most heroic unconcern, a journey of nearly three thousand miles, through such difficulties as it is easy for us to imagine, and leaving a letter to La Salle, as a proof of his visit, in the same way that one would, in these degenerate days of effeminacy, leave a card at a neighbor's house.

The French extended their explorations up to the mouth of the Red River. On their return the two brothers separated when they arrived at Bayou Manchac. Bienville was ordered to go down the river to the French fleet, to give information of what they had seen and heard. Iberville went through Bayou Manchac to those lakes which are known under the names of Pontchartrain and Maurepas. Louisiana had been named from a king: was it not in keeping that those lakes should be called after ministers?

From the Bay of St. Louis, Iberville returned to his fleet, where, after consultation, he determined to make a settlement at the Bay of Biloxi. On the east side, at the mouth of the bay, as it were, there is a slight swelling of the shore, about four acres square, sloping gently to the woods in the background, and on the bay. Thus this position was fortified by nature, and the French skilfully availed themselves of these advantages. The weakest point, which was on the side of the forest, they strengthened with more care than the rest, by connecting with a strong intrenchment the two ravines, which ran to the bay in a parallel line to each other. The fort was constructed with four bastions, and was armed with twelve pieces of artillery. . . .

A few huts having been erected round the fort, the settlers began to clear the land, in order to bring it into cultivation. Iberville having furnished them with all the necessary provisions, utensils, and other supplies, prepared to sail for France. . . . As the country had been ordered to be explored, Sauvolle availed himself of that circumstance to refresh the minds of his men by the excitement of an expedition into the interior of the continent. He therefore hastened to dispatch most of them with Bienville, who, with a chief of the Bayagoulas for his guide, went to visit the Colapissas. They inhabited the northern shore of Lake Pontchartrain, and their domains embraced the sites now occupied by Lewisburg, Mandeville, and Fontainebleau. . . .

Iberville had been gone for several months, and the year was drawing to a close without any tidings of him. A deeper gloom had settled over the little colony at Biloxi, when, on December 7th, some signal-guns were heard at sea, and the grateful sound came booming over the waters, spreading joy in every breast. . . . It was Iberville returning with the news that, on his representations, Sauvolle had been appointed by the King governor of Louisiana; Bienville, lieutenant-governor; and Boisbriant, commander of the fort at Biloxi, with the grade of major. Iberville, having been informed by Bienville of the attempt of the English to make a settlement on the banks of the Mississippi, and of the manner in which it had been foiled, resolved to take precautionary measures against the repetition of any similar attempt. Without loss of time he departed with Bienville, on January 16, 1700, and running up the river, he constructed a small fort, on the first solid ground which he met, and which is said to have been at a distance of fifty-four miles from its mouth.

When so engaged the two brothers one day saw a canoe rapidly sweeping down the river and approaching the spot where they stood. It was occupied by eight men, six of whom were rowers, the seventh was the steersman, and the eighth, from his appearance, was evidently of a superior order to that of his companions, and the commander of the party. Well may it be imagined what greeting the stranger received, when leaping on shore he made himself known as the Chevalier de Tonty, who had again heard of the establishment of a colony in Louisiana, and who, for the second time, had come to see if there was any truth in the report. With what emotion did Iberville and Bienville fold in their arms the faithful companion and friend of La Salle, of whom they had heard so many wonderful tales from the Indians, to whom he was so well known under the name of "Iron Hand!" With what admiration they looked at his person, and with what increasing interest they listened to his long recitals of what he had done and had seen on that broad continent, the threshold of which they had hardly passed!

After having rested three days at the fort, the indefatigable Tonty reascended the Mississippi, with Iberville and Bienville, and finally parted with them at Natchez. Iberville was so much pleased with that part of the bank of the river where now exists the city of Natchez that he marked it down as a most eligible spot for a town, of which he drew the plan, and which he called Rosalie, after the maiden name of the Countess Pontchartrain, the wife of the chancellor. He then returned to the new fort he was erecting on the Mississippi, and Bienville went to explore the country of the Yatasses, of the Natchitoches, and of the Ouachitas. What romance can be more agreeable to the imagination than to accompany Iberville and Bienville in their wild explorations, and to compare the state of the country in their time with what it is in our days? . . .

After these explorations Iberville departed again for France, to solicit additional assistance from the government, and left Bienville in command of the new fort on the Mississippi. It was very hard for the two brothers, Sauvolle and Bienville, to be thus separated, when they stood so much in need of each other's countenance, to breast the difficulties that sprung up around them with a luxuriance which they seemed to borrow from the vegetation of the country. The distance between the Mississippi and Biloxi was not so easily overcome in those days as in ours, and the means which the two brothers had of communing together were very scanty and uncertain.

Sauvolle died August 22, 1701, and Louisiana remained under the sole charge of Bienville, who, tho very young, was fully equal to meet that emergency, by the maturity of his mind and by his other qualifications. He had hardly consigned his brother to the tomb when Iberville returned with two ships of the line and a brig laden with troops and provisions.

According to Iberville's orders, and in conformity with the King's instructions, Bienville left Boisbriant, his cousin, with twenty men, at the old fort of Biloxi, and transported the principal seat of the colony to the western side of the river Mobile, not far from the spot where now stands the city of Mobile. Near the mouth of that river there is an island, which the French had called Massacre Island from the great quantity of human bones which they found bleaching on its shores. It was evident that there some awful tragedy had been acted; but Tradition, when interrogated, laid her choppy fingers upon her skinny lips, and answered not. . . .

The year 1703 slowly rolled by and gave way to 1704. Still, nothing was heard from the parent country. There seemed to be an impassable barrier between the old and the new continent. The milk which flowed from the motherly breast of France could no longer reach the parched lips of her new-born infant; and famine began to pinch the colonists, who scattered themselves all along the coast, to live by fishing. They were reduced to the veriest extremity of misery, and despair had settled in every bosom, in spite of the encouragements of Bienville, who displayed the most manly fortitude amid all the trials to which he was subjected. . . .

Iberville had not been able to redeem his pledge to the poor colonists, but he sent his brother Chateaugué in his place, at the imminent risk of being captured by the English, who occupied, at that time, most of the avenues of the Gulf of Mexico. He was not the man to spare either himself or his family in cases of emergency, and his heroic soul was inured to such sacrifices. Grateful the colonists were for this act of devotedness, and they resumed the occupation of their tenements which they had abandoned in search of food. The aspect of things was suddenly changed; abundance and hope reappeared in the land, whose population was increased by the arrival of seventeen persons, who came, under the guidance of Chateaugué, with the intention of making a permanent settlement, and who had provided themselves with all the implements of husbandry.

This excitement had hardly subsided when it was revived by the appearance of another ship, and it became intense when the inhabitants saw a procession of twenty females, with veiled faces, proceeding arm in arm, and two by two, to the house of the Governor, who received them in state and provided them with suitable lodgings. What did it mean? The next morning, which was Sunday, the mystery was cleared by the officiating priest reading from the pulpit, after mass, and for the general information, the following communication from the minister to Bienville:

"His majesty sends twenty girls to be married to the Canadians and to the other inhabitants of Mobile, in order to consolidate the colony. All these girls are industrious and have received a pious and virtuous education. You will take care to settle them in life as well as may be in your power, and to marry them to such men as are capable of providing them with a commodious home."

Many were the gibes and high was the glee on that occasion; pointed were the jokes aimed at young Bienville on his being thus transformed into a matrimonial agent and *pater familiæ*. The intentions of the King, however, were faithfully executed, and more than one rough but honest Canadian boatman of the St. Lawrence and of the Mississippi closed his adventurous and erratic career and became a domestic and useful member of that little commonwealth, under the watchful influence of the dark-eyed maid of the Loire or of the Seine.

OGLETHORPE IN GEORGIA

(1733)

BY JOEL CHANDLER HARRIS[1]

General James Edward Oglethorpe, the founder
of the Colony of Georgia, was among the few
really good and great men that history tells us of.
We need to keep a close eye on the antics of history. She places the laurels of fame in the hands
of butchers, plunderers, and adventurers, and even
assassins share her favors; so that, if we are
going to enjoy the feast that history offers us,
we must not inquire too closely into the characters
of the men whom she makes heroes of. We find,
when we come to look into the matter, that but
few of those who figured as the great men of the
world have been entirely unselfish; and unselfish-
ness is the test of a man who is really good and
great. Judged by this test, General Oglethorpe
stands among the greatest men known to history. . . .

Born in 1689, Oglethorpe entered the English
army when twenty-one years of age. In 1714 he
became captain-lieutenant of the first troop of the
Queen's life guards. He shortly afterward joined
Eugene on the continent, and remained with that
soldier until the peace of 1718. On the death of
his brother he succeeded to the family estate in

---

[1] From Mr. Harris's "Georgia from the Invasion of De
Soto to Recent Times." By permission of, and by arrangement with, the publishers, D. Appleton & Co. Copyright,
1899.

England. In 1722 he was elected to Parliament from Haslemere, County of Surrey, and this borough he represented continuously for thirty-two years. His parliamentary career was marked by wise prudence and consistency; and his sympathies were warmly enlisted for the relief of unfortunate soldiers, and in securing reform in the conduct of prisons. In this way Oglethorpe became a philanthropist, and, without intending it, attracted the attention of all England. Pope, the poet, eulogizes his "strong benevolence of soul."

In that day and time men were imprisoned for debt in England. The law was brutal, and those who executed it were cruel. There was no discrimination between fraud and misfortune. The man who was unable to pay his debts was judged to be as criminal as the man who, though able, refused to pay. . . .

This condition of affairs Oglethorpe set himself to reform; and while thus engaged he became imprest with the idea that many of the unfortunates, guilty of no crime, and of respectable connections, might benefit themselves, relieve England of the shame of their imprisonment, and confirm and extend the dominion of the mother country in the New World, by being freed from the claims of those to whom they owed money, on condition that they would consent to become colonists in America. To this class were to be added recruits from those who, through lack of work and of means, were likely to be imprisoned on account of their misfortunes. Oglethorpe was also of the opinion that men of means, enterprise, and ambition could be enlisted in the cause; and in this he was not mistaken.

He had no hope whatever of personal gain or private benefit. The plan that he had conceived was entirely for the benefit of the unfortunate, based on broad and high ideas of benevolence; and so thoroughly was this understood that Oglethorpe had no difficulty whatever in securing the aid of men of wealth and influence. A charter or grant from the government was applied for, in order that the scheme might have the sanction and authority of the government. Accordingly a charter was granted, and the men most prominent in the scheme of benevolence were incorporated under the name of "The Trustees for establishing the Colony of Georgia in America." Georgia in America was, under the terms of the charter, a pretty large slice of America. It embraced all that part of the continent lying between the Savannah and Altamaha rivers, and extending westly from the heads of these rivers in direct lines to the South Seas; so that the original territory of Georgia extended from ocean to ocean.

In aid of this enterprise, Oglethorpe not only contributed largely from his private means, and solicited contributions from his wealthy friends, but wrote a tract in which he used arguments that were practical as well as ingenious.

On the 17th of November, 1732, all arrangements having been completed, the *Anne* set sail for the Colony of Georgia, accompanied by Oglethorpe, who furnished his own cabin, and laid in provisions not only for himself, but for his fellow-passengers. On the 13th of January, 1733, the *Anne* anchored in Charleston harbor. From Charleston the vessel sailed to Port Royal; and the colonists were soon quartered in the barracks of Beaufort-town, which had been prepared for their reception. Oglethorpe left the colonists at Beaufort and, in company with Colonel William Bull, proceeded to the Savannah River. He went up this stream as far as Yamacraw Bluff, which he selected as the site of the settlement he was about to make. He marked out the town, and named it Savannah. The site was a beautiful one in Oglethorpe's day, and it is still more beautiful now. The little settlement that the founder of the colony marked out has grown into a flourishing city, and art has added its advantages to those of nature to make Savannah one of the most beautiful cities in the United States. . . .

On the 30th of January, 1733, the immigrants set sail from Beaufort, and on the afternoon of the next day they arrived at Yamacraw Bluff. On the site of the town that had already been marked off they pitched four tents large enough to accommodate all the people. Oglethorpe, after posting his sentinels, slept on the ground under the shelter of the tall pines, near the central watch fire. As a soldier should, he slept soundly. He had planted the new colony, and thus far all had gone well with him and with those whose interests he had charge of.

To bring these colonists across the ocean and place them in a position where they might begin life anew was not a very difficult undertaking; but to plant a colony amongst savages already suspicious of the whites, and to succeed in obtaining their respect, friendship, and aid, was something that required wisdom, courage, prudence, and large experience. This Oglethorpe did; and it is to his credit that, during the time he had charge of the colony, he never, in any shape or form, took advantage of the ignorance of the Indians. His method of dealing with them was very simple. He conciliated them by showing them that the whites could be just, fair, and honorable in their dealings; and thus, in the very beginning, he won the friendship of those whose enmity to the little colony would have proved ruinous.

Providence favored Oglethorpe in this matter. He had to deal with an Indian chief full of years, wisdom, and experience. This was Tomochichi, who was at the head of the Yamacraws. From this kindly Indian the Georgia Colony received untold benefits. He remained the steadfast friend of the settlers, and used his influence in their behalf in every possible way, and on all occasions. Altho he was a very old man, he was strong and active, and of commanding presence. He possessed remarkable intelligence; and this, added to his experience, made him one of the most remarkable of the Indians whose names have been preserved in history. . . . Thus, with Oglethorpe to direct it, and with Tomochichi as its friend, the little Georgia Colony was founded, thrived and flourished.

END OF VOL. II